Eye to Eye

Eye to Eye

A Memoir

Cyril Frankel

as tolfd tp

Henry Cobbold

BANK HOUSE BOOKS

First published in the United Kingdom in 2010 by

Bank House Books

PO Box 3

NEW ROMNEY

TN29 9WJ UK

www.bankhousebooks.com

British Library Cataloguing in Publication Data
A catalogue record for this book is available from the British Library

ISBN 9781904408604

Typesetting and origination by Bank House Books
Printed by Lightning Source

Contents

Foreword by Henry Cobbold

Cyril Frankel. Born 1921. Died 1973. Or so Leslie Halliwell's *Filmgoer's Companion, Eighth Edition, 1985* would have us believe. Halliwell's *Eighth Edition* also tells us that Cyril Frankel directed a film two years after he died, *Permission to Kill*, in 1975. Listed after *Permission to Kill*, at the end of a list of feature titles dating back to the early 1950s, is a tantalising 'etc.'.

I telephone the Director's Guild of Great Britain. 'Yes, Cyril Frankel. We haven't heard from him in a while, but we have an address here . . . in Harley Street.' Harley Street! I had a vision of a medical facility with a director in a tank, technically dead but still able to raise his finger for 'Action!'

This was 1985, and – inspired by Max Ophuls's *Letter from an Unknown Woman* (1947) – I had written my first screenplay, a country house melodrama for actress Joan Fontaine. How to tempt Joan Fontaine from apparent retirement in northern California? Looking at Joan's filmography, I saw that the last feature film she made was in England, in 1966: *The Witches*, directed by Cyril Frankel. The only time she had left America to work since then was in 1980 for a play in Vienna, *The Lion in Winter* . . . directed by Cyril Frankel.

I send my screenplay to northern California and to Harley Street, and within a week I receive replies from both saying they would like to make the film. Echoing the drama of many of the stories in this book, the film didn't happen – but it was the beginning of two beautiful friendships.

Cyril's Harley Street apartment is not large, but it has high ceilings and tall walls and these give the clues to a lifetime of stories – pots by Lucie Rie; paintings by Martin Bloch; photos of Maharishi and of Ava Gardner; VHS cassettes of television screenings of *Alive and Kicking* and *It's Great to Be Young*; shiny new DVD box sets of *Randall and Hopkirk* and *The Baron*; filing cabinets overspilling with photos, clippings, letters . . .

It is in this treasure trove, to a background of whistling taxi cabs and clanking scaffold poles through the raised sash windows, that Cyril has told me the story that is contained within these pages. It is the tale of many lifetimes, spanning many countries, many characters, many disappointments and many triumphs in many different fields. It is an extraordinary twentieth-century tale that continues on into the twenty-first . . . despite Leslie Halliwell's attempts to cut it short.

What follows is what was missing when Halliwell typed 'etc.'.

Henry Cobbold
October 2008

Foreword by Alexandra Bastedo

I suppose it could be said that I owe my life as it is to Cyril Frankel. He was very much the man who 'discovered' me, trained me in the ways of film acting and ultimately launched me.

How did it happen? I had secretly done a campaign for Shell petrol of Europe – minus England as at that time it was not the 'done thing' for actresses to model. However, ironically a friend of Cyril's in Germany told him about this English girl whom he had seen splashed across the billboards of Europe dressed entirely in white leather and holding the nozzle of a petrol pump!

It just so happened that Cyril, who was to be the main director of the forthcoming ATV series *The Champions,* was looking for an actress to co-star with two male leads. Thus I found myself doing a film test alongside Suart Damon and William Gaunt. Much to our surprise, the chemistry worked and we were all cast in the leading roles of Craig Stirling, Richard Barrett and Sharron Macready.

Filming thirty episodes of one hour each, back to back over the period of one year and three months, proved to be an exciting if gruelling experience. Without the gentle but firm presence of Cyril Frankel I doubt whether I would have survived it. I was a mere novice at the age of twwenty, straight from the Brighton School of Drama and the Derby Repertory Theatre. Although *The Champions* was a TV series it was not taped – which was usually the case in those days – but filmed. So it was film technique that I had to learn very quickly under Cyril's guidance: how to hit my mark, how to act in close-up as opposed to long shot, how to be aware of camera angles and how to stay within the boundaries of the flattering lighting designed specifically for my face by the lighting designer under Cyril's guidance – all in addition to the performance itself!

Cyril turned the series into a class act and it was sold all over the world. It has been repeated endlessly and continues to be seen somewhere every week.

I still remember my first meeting with Cyril, who struck me as being a very spiritual person. I was very shy, but his kindness shone through and he soon put me at my ease. Strong but gentle, reserved but enthusiastic, serious but with a sense of humour, kind but determined, and highly artistic and literary, with a love of music – Cyril possesses all the qualities of a first class director.

It is hardly surprising that he has had such a fabulous showbiz career and it is wonderful to be able to read all about it in his book. It should also be said that he is much loved by all those who have worked for him and is an exceptional man.

Once again my thanks to Cyril for changing my life.

Alexandra Bastedo

Preface

We all experience the touch of one hand to another, which can communicate not only the physical state of the partner but can develop into the confirmation of love. Eye to Eye is the pathway that facilitates contact between the deeper levels of individual minds. It is acknowledged in Spanish – *'hasta la vista'*, in German – *'auf wiedersehen'* and in French – *'au revoir'*.

Of course in the twentieth century Eye to Eye has been relevant in cinema, particularly in the close-up, where the camera expresses the emotional response through the eye – illustrated by the fame of Garbo, the suggestiveness of Mae West and the world appreciation of Marilyn.

The journey from Eye to Eye passes through the channels of emotional response from individual to individual.

Cyril Frankel

Chapter 1

Family Background

I was born lucky. Accordingly to my mother, Hannah, I readily popped out into the world. Curly dark hair. Blue eyes. Soon wanting to entertain.

I came into the world on 28 December, three days after Christmas 1921, at 23 Lordship Park, Stoke Newington. Both my parents' families lived close by. My grandparents on my father's side lived just round the corner in Queen Elizabeth's Walk. I went round there a lot, because the family was Jewish and my grandparents celebrated religious holidays as a way of bringing everyone together. My mother's family lived probably half a mile away, until they moved into our house at no. 23 when we moved to a bigger house up the road at no. 37. So we were all within minutes of one another, including uncles and aunts on my father's side, who all lived in the neighbourhood. Our new house had a nice garden, several fruit trees and a vegetable garden at the back of the lawn.

Lordship Park was off Green Lanes, which was a road (along which trams ran) that went up to Manor House and then on to Harringay. The road was called Lordship Park, but the park itself was called Clissold Park, and that was about 100 yards away from our house. Clissold Park had a bandstand as well as wonderful animals: deer and stags and birds. Finsbury Park, which was larger, wasn't far away either, with its pond and rowing boats, and, very importantly, its bandstand. It was quite a genteel part of London at this time.

Up near Manor House there was the Sir John of Beverley Institute for the Deaf and Dumb, and attached to that a kindergarten run by Madame Cartwright, a French lady, and her very charming daughter. It was she who first encouraged me to draw and paint, and I have happy recollections of my time there. Then I went to another school in Green Lanes, called St John's College, until I went to Highgate. St John's was OK, although the rather sadistic headmaster used to make holes in doors so he could spy on pupils. In those days, London was relatively crime-free, and from the age of four I walked alone to kindergarten, which was a good half a mile away. Parents didn't worry about this. It was different; very different. The only outsiders, I suppose, were gypsies, but they were more fascinating than anything else; we weren't frightened of them. They came knocking on your door to read your hand, to tell your fortune, not to steal your children.

I told you I was born at no. 23. At no. 21, next door, lived a couple, well into middle age, fifty perhaps, if not older. The husband had a spade beard, wore a top hat, and his name was Gestetner: he was the inventor of the first duplicating machine. There were a lot of other interesting people in that street, and we got to know them all, in addition to our relatives. At the weekend we used to have parties; it was a very very sociable life. I regret that this kind of scene seems to have slipped away from London now. People had open doors and open hearts. It was a civilised life.

My earliest memory – apart from the natural ones of enjoying breast-feeding and all that! – is the passing of my great-grandmother, on my mother's side, in the winter of 1924. My great-grandmother had had nine children. Her husband had died relatively young, but she lived to within weeks of being a hundred. When she was in her nineties the *Daily Mirror* published a whole page about her dancing, smoking and penchant for whisky. My parents said they thought I was too young to go to a funeral, so I stayed at home and upset everybody by putting up an umbrella up in the house. This was supposed to be unlucky – and I remember there was a great flash of lightning.

My great-grandmother's name was Levy; her family had been in England since the fifteenth century. She lived at first in Birmingham, but struggled on her own to earn enough to bring up all those children. So she came down to London, and became the licensee of a pub called the Marquis of Granby: in that way she was able to support her family. My grandfather, Lewis Levy, was one of her sons and my mother was her grandchild.

As they grew up, several of the nine children and many grandchildren spread around the world, including Great-Uncle Harry to Australia and Ralph to South Africa. Priscilla opened a bridge and poker club in Cazenove Road, Stoke Newington, while Beatrice married Henry (known as Harry) Lesser, who built cinemas; they lived somewhere up Cricklewood way. Beatrice and Harry's daughters, Lenny and Violet, became actresses who starred at the Theatre Royal, Drury Lane, in a musical called *Wild Violets*. They were both beautiful and talented, though very different.

My mother had a cousin called Monty Misell, and as a youth I became friendly with his two children, Warren and Betty. Warren was surprisingly undemonstrative as a youth but as he grew older that changed. He revised his surname, becoming Warren Mitchell – and later became the celebrated Alf Garnett, an altogether warm and friendly guy. I notice as I write that he is receiving rave reviews for Arthur Miller's *The Price*.

The Levys were quite different from my father's family, who'd only come to England probably in the 1880s, when my father was about six. The family had been extremely well established in a town called Chemiche, which is now part of Poland but was then part of Austria-Hungary. My grandmother lived in a great castle, and I think it was her brother or her father – I'm not sure – who was the local burgomeister, similar to an English mayor. There was a stock market crash, and my grandparents came to England because another member of the family had already arrived and said the streets were paved with gold. Growing up, my father inherited the wish of his parents that he should rebuild the family's fortunes. He worked in the fur industry, very successfully. Doing a lot with the Hudson Bay Company, he was also involved in a lot of charitable work – both for an orphanage and also as founder and chairman of the Fur Trade and Widows Benevolent Society.

My grandfather was more of a poet than a businessman: his name was Leopold Frankel (thus my younger sister, who is no longer with us, was called Leonora). My grandfather always called me Squirrel – 'where's my Squirrel?' My father's mother was Rose, a very strong character. This side of the family believed very much in academic achievements, and my grandmother Rose always encouraged me to study.

To outward appearances my father's family was more religious than my mother's, but this didn't stop us having things like bacon for breakfast. When we celebrated religious festivals, eating wonderful food, we were sometimes joined by people I hardly knew, cousins, uncles or great-uncles. One uncle, named Bard, was married to my father's eldest sister, Nita. Their son Basil became a very important lawyer, and was in line to be attorney general. His younger brother was a top accountant. Glamour came from my mother's side of the family – and this is what gave me the desire to express myself in the world of entertainment. At the end of large family dinners a cousin or two and I always put on a show. I had a talent for mimicry, which didn't always go down well if I imitated people who were sitting around the table. This gift was a help to me later, during my Army career – when I moved on from imitating film stars to Churchill and Neville Chamberlain.

We were four children: Violet, Leslie, Leonora and me. Only two of us are left: Violet, who's had a series of mini strokes recently, and me. She has three children, Richard, Michael and Louise; her husband, Jack, died very young, in his forties.

My mother's brother Mark, who had a showroom in Moorgate, turned out lady's handbags which were on sale in all the top London stores. He did pretty well and he was very generous. If you went up there at Christmas he would open a drawer and give you a watch or something else nice. He married late in life when he'd already retired. In those days Jewish people married Jewish people, and as his girlfriend wasn't Jewish he hadn't married her – but when he finally decided to everybody was so pleased. It was kind of a secret life that they'd had, and he always lamented that he should have got married much earlier. They lived for a while in the West Hampstead, Willesden area, and then moved to Harley Street. In later years my friend Steve Nelson used to go and look after Uncle Mark, who was a great whisky drinker – always Black Label. If you went down there at half past nine in the morning he'd say, 'I'll pour you a Scotch.' You'd say, 'Oh no, it's too early,' and he'd reply, 'Don't be silly.' Steve said it was because he was lonely – because his wife had died by then, and they had no children – and if he got somebody down there he wanted to keep them as long as possible!

During the war my parents moved to Hampstead Garden Suburb. From there, towards the end of the war, they moved to

Park Lane, to a big flat facing the park. This sounds grand, but it was rented for £14 a week. When the landlords put the rent up my father wasn't at all happy, so we moved to a flat in George Street, in a very nice block, for about £15 a week. But that was expensive: in those days, I'm talking 1945, '46, £6 a week for a flat was quite a lot of money. After all, when I got my first job in 1946 I didn't *earn* £6 a week!

Chapter 2

Childhood 1921–1937

I directed my first show at the house I was born in, in the attic, aged about eight. I placed a string across the room and hung two sheets from it with safety pins. Local kids came along and we did a revue; their parents and our neighbours were the audience. My father and mother were always into charities, and I had to do something to help so I put on a show. I made 7s 2d for the local orphanage by selling sweets in the interval to the audience.

A great influence on me and my siblings was our Cornish nanny, Henrietta Lelean – we knew her as Nurse – who was with us for eighteen years. She was a wonderful lady, and we all really adored her. She had her own, very strong character. She never married, but I think she had a pretty full life – particularly in the early days, before she came to us. Her father had been a sea captain: his name was Lean, and he was apparently so courageous that the French called him Le Lean; so the family name became Lelean.

Nurse had a brother whom she admired very much – he did a lot of watercolours, of which I have one or two – but she didn't get on with his wife. So she came up to London and became a family nurse, first for a family in Highgate and then for us. Falmouth was her home town, and she knew all the little villages and towns in that part of Cornwall very well. This is why we went down there for summer holidays – for the whole of August – while my parents did their own thing, going to Nice or wherever! They never came to Cornwall with us, but in my earlier days we had holidays with my parents at Margate, Clacton and Bognor. Nurse rented an apartment for us in Falmouth and we made trips to interesting places. She introduced us to all the Cornish foods – of which there were many, not just Cornish cream teas but hog's pudding (a cross between a pate and a liver sausage), saffron cake and 'heavy cake'. Every Friday evening a small bus went on a 'mystery tour': you paid your shilling and you might end up at the Lizard or Lands End or Port Isaac or Mousehole. And I made many friends. Many friends. It really began because on the main beach there – Gyllyngvase beach – there were rented huts: you'd meet the people in the next hut, and then the next one, and you ended up meeting them year after year. They might be locals like the Truscott family, who were the butchers in the area, or Colonel Curnow, who suffered from tuberculosis. He talked to me, and introduced me to a magazine called *Psychic News*.

Psychic News was run by a spiritualist, which got me interested in the idea of the psychic world, particularly as I'd seen a film with Ann Harding and Gary Cooper – *Peter Ibbetson* – which was about people meeting in their dreams. It appealed to me. Little did I know that in years to come I would become the chairman of the organisation that published *Psychic News* – by chance, not by choice. It no longer exists.

There was a girl called Joan Wright whom I was very fond of. Her mother was a wonderful cook, and used to cook enormous Cornish pasties especially for me. The family had a lovely house in Redruth, where I would visit them. Unfortunately the father, who was a big man – really big – got involved in investments and lost all his money. His wife woke up one night, couldn't see where he was, until she saw hands hanging onto the window sill. Then he fell . . . and, being a very big man, he died. She was left penniless. Joan was so upset that she became a nun for two or three years; and her mother rented the house out as bedsits. Unfortunately, with the war, and travel, and life going on, I lost touch. But we had lots of lovely times down there.

We didn't always stay in the same place, until towards the end when we stayed on several occasions at 69 Marlborough Road in Falmouth. It was at this time I became very friendly with a girl named Eleanor and a friend of hers, Marie. We used to go to barn dances in St Mawes together, and had a whale of a time.

I was an encyclopaedia of film at this time, fascinated by it. I was seduced by the glamour of cinemas, enthralled by the musical hall timing of films such as *The Golddiggers* of 1933. I remember in one day I saw *The Last of the Mohicans* at the London Pavilion, *Marie Walewska* with Greta Garbo and Charles Boyer at the Empire [probably *Conquest*, 1937 - Ed], then *The Great Ziegfield* – a three and a half hour epic – at the London Hippodrome.

I was lucky to have parents who loved theatre and music hall, as well as cinema as it learnt to speak (it was silent films at first, of course). In the last chapter I mentioned the Lesser family and my two glamorous cousins, the Dean sisters. The Lessers owned the Astoria chain – there were the Brixton Astoria, the Streatham Astoria and the Finsbury Park Astoria – of which Finsbury Park was the most spectacular. I can't tell you how impressive it was. You entered the most glorious – what would you call it – it wasn't just a foyer, because in the centre it had a wonderful fountain, surrounded by water with lots of goldfish. And all around on the first floor there was a restaurant: you went through there and through another hall before you entered the cinema. And that was huge, with a big circle area, resembling a Spanish castle. There were balconies, and the lighting gave the effect of clouds scuttling across a night sky lit with stars. Some years back, when I made a television film with Eartha Kitt, I chose to film there, and it still had its magic; it still had its sparkling stars in the ceiling.

I became so interested in cinema architecture that every time a new cinema opened I had to make a special trip on the trams to see what the décor was like. But the Finsbury Park Astoria remained the finest. I remember a very pretty blonde girl in one of the two box offices, who I got to know because I became such a regular visitor – her name was Muriel Ainge. Then there was John, the uniformed commissionaire. Because I was such a regular fan they treated me well, once they got to know me, giving me complimentary tickets on special occasions.

My parents were so involved with each other, and with their theatre-going and bridge and poker clubs, that I could get away with a lot. I had my little pocket money, and to go to the cinema locally was only about 6*d* in those days. To put this in context, a newspaper was only 1*d*. A bus ride was 1*d* as well, so even as a child you could move around – and my travels gradually came to encompass the West End cinemas. I was very fond of the Empire at Leicester Square, an MGM cinema. One of the very first films that I eventually made had its première there, which meant a great deal to me.

I remember aged about eleven wanting to go and see a film called *Tom Sawyer,* which was on at the Plaza in Piccadilly Circus. I took the Underground from Finsbury Park to Piccadilly Circus and went up to the box office – I think it was 1*s* 6*d* to get in – and the girl said, 'Sorry, you have to be sixteen to come in.' I replied that *Tom Sawyer* was a U certificate. 'Yes, but there's also a film with Clara Bow, called *Kick In,* which has an A certificate, so you can't go in alone. You either have to go in with an adult or not at all.' The woman behind me in the queue said, 'Oh, I'll take him in.' And she did. There wasn't much wrong with Clara Bow; she was rather an attractive and curvaceous lady. Anyhow I saw the films, and there was a stage show as well. That's a thing that used to happen at Finsbury Park Astoria, where they had a Wurlitzer that rose from the floor and a large revolving stage; there were quite spectacular stage shows for about half an hour between two movies. You got a lot of value for your 1*s* 6*d* or 6*d* or whatever. So I saw this film, *Kick In,* but at home nobody believed that I'd been to the West End until I did some drawings of the stage show – and that convinced them!

The cinema became a huge influence in my life. I used to challenge schoolfriends to ask me any question about any film, who was in it or who directed it, and generally I came up with the right answer. My parents also enjoyed the cinema. They also, I'm happy to say, enjoyed the music hall. Locally we had the Finsbury Park Empire, which changed its programme every week: it might be Gracie Fields, or Will Hay, or some big American orchestra like Cab Calloway or Duke Ellington. My parents would say to me, 'Would you go and get us two tickets?' I'd reply, 'No, I'll get you three.' I learnt a lot about comedy and timing from the music hall. It seems clear to me that television today has reduced communication between performer and audience, so that actors, particularly comedians, are less practised at the art of timing.

One Saturday evening when I was at Highgate School I wanted to go to the cinema, but when I looked at the evening paper I had seen all the films – as well as anything I wanted to see at the theatre. And then I saw, under opera and ballet, 'Sadler's Wells: *Madame Butterfly*'. I had seen a film called *One Night of Love,* which starred an opera singer called Grace Moore, a really lovely woman, who had a glorious voice and sang 'One Fine Day' from *Madame Butterfly*, which touched me very much – so I thought, ooh, I'll go to the opera, thinking it was bound to be easy to get in. To my surprise, when I got there it was House Full; standing room only. Then I discovered the company had a repertoire: the following Saturday it was *Marriage of Figaro*, then it might be *La Bohème* or *Rigoletto*.

I was hooked. On a school day I'd go home when school finished at half-past four, have a bite to eat, run down the road again, and jump on a tram from Green Lanes down to the Angel Islington. Then after the show I'd walk back, stopping for fish and chips from a newspaper en route. I got a tram, then walked on to Sadler's Wells. There, if you stood in a queue outside the gallery by, I think it was eight o'clock or quarter past, for 6*d* you could have a stool reservation for the gallery. The thing was to get near the front of the queue. All I needed to be careful of in the gallery was not to take Miss Pilgrim's seat. Miss Pilgrim had a sweetshop near King's Cross. She was a great lover of opera and Shakespeare, and she queued up every night. At the end of the performance she always stood forward and sang 'God Save The King' louder than anyone else in the theatre. Eventually Lillian Baylis, who founded the Old Vic and Sadler's Wells, gave her a reserved seat in the unreserved gallery, so she didn't need to queue: she could just come in. And of course on an early visit I went and sat in her seat all unwittingly; and there she was, saying, 'That's *my* seat!' We soon became good friends and she educated me a lot about the singers and the operas, who had done this and sung that. I visited her one time at her sweet shop when she was ill. Such a character. Yes, her spirit lives on.

It was my cousin Gerald, with whom I'd more or less been brought up, who encouraged me to go the ballet: Colonel De Basil's Russian Ballet at Drury Lane. And yes, I quite enjoyed it, but I was still full of opera. I wasn't particularly taken by the Russian Ballet, except for *Prince Igor*, which was quite exciting. And then the daughter of the landlady where we had stayed on holiday in Cornwall came to London and insisted on going to the ballet instead of the opera. That time it happened to be rather a good performance, and I was captivated then.

We were taken to the theatre on school trips. I remember being taken to the Old Vic to see Ralph Richardson as Othello, with Laurence Olivier as Iago. I was star struck. My first encounter with a star was with the wonderful Sophie Tucker, star of *Life Begins at Forty*. My parents were on their way back from a business trip to America, and my father met her playing bridge. When I went to Waterloo to meet the boat train I remember there was an actress called Sally Eilers, as popular as any of the Hollywood stars, getting off the train . . . and then I was introduced to Sophie Tucker.

Later, in the '60s, I went to see Sophie Tucker's last appearance in London, at the Dominion, at the top of the Variety bill. As well as being a big star she was a big woman, and always had this tremendous 'red hot momma' image. She gave a terrific performance. I went back stage and asked if she remembered my parents and so on, and she did. She was very nice, but she said, 'I just can't do this twice a night; I just can't do it any more,' and she was shaking. All her money went into an orphanage she created. She was a wonderful lady.

At Highgate School I connived and cheated in order to see every film rather than be involved in sport or other activities. It's said you enjoy what you're good at. I did enjoy and was good at running the 440 yards (there were the 100 yards, the 220 and the 440), cross country and at Eton fives. It was through running that I met my lifetime friend and future editor Alvin Bailey. He was about three or four years younger than me – which was an enormous gap in those days, when I was sixteen or so. I was just setting off on a cross country run when he said, 'I'll hold your blazer for you.' Off I went, down West Hill and across Kenwood, and when I came back he introduced himself. I was invited back to his house for tea and to meet his family. Alvin's father was a tailor, and after the war he made my first suit for £9.

I actually won a mug, a pewter mug, for fives. It's a wonderful story. There was a guy who was brilliant at the game, called Laurence, and when we were picked out to play together he said to me, 'You're not to hit the ball.' I just went from side to side and he played. We won and went on to the next round, then the next round. Somewhere or other I have that mug, won without hitting a single ball! No, I lie: I hit the ball once, and he said, 'I told you *not* to hit the ball!'

I was a day boy, but there were boarders as well. It was a good school. When I first went there the headmaster was Dr Johnston, and he was a great figure of a man with a flowing gown: he had a tremendous personality. By the time I went to

Oxford he had died, but his very lovely widow was living at East Gate Hotel on the High; I used to go and have tea with her. It was a nice link.

My French master at Highgate was Jean Neurohr, known as 'Nero'. Every Friday evening he took a group of about six of us to Soho to educate us about London and food. I must have been about fourteen. Soho was quite different in those days from how it is now: it was simply a place you went to for a meal. Whereas every street has two or three Italian restaurants these days, there was only one in London then, and it was in Soho. It didn't even have an Italian name – it was called Café Bleu. For 1s 6d you could have spaghetti bolognese. We also went to the one Chinese restaurant in Soho, Leons, and a Greek restaurant in Lower Shaftesbury Avenue, called Demos.

It was on these occasions that I came to meet Nero's wife, Lillian, who was Irish and stunningly beautiful. She introduced me to short stories by Katherine Mansfield, and to the drawings and paintings of Gaudier Breska. It was an entry into a sophisticated world. Lillian also took me to Soho, and introduced me to Café Ann, in St Giles High Street, where we went for a coffee. This was where prostitutes hung out; the glamour of it appealed to me. I became very friendly with a girl called Lucinda, one of the prostitutes . . . but the glamour of it. It was the glamour of it.

Lillian wouldn't call me Cyril; she would only call me Solomon, my middle name. She used to invite me for tea at 4.30, when school finished, for conversation. Ironically she also invited a chap called Wilkinson from time to time, who was a fascist and a bully. During the war he ended up in the Tower because he was such an active member of Mosley's Blackshirts.

Nero became French Ambassador to Poland and Lillian went there with him. Many years later she returned to England, but I saw her only once. By then she was rather a sad elderly lady and she didn't have much money. I think her husband had passed on, and she was in pretty rough circumstances, but she had a daughter, Elizabeth, and was looking for somewhere to live.

I'd heard she was in London from Wilkinson's brother. When he sought me out he told me his brother was still in Highgate, and gave me the address. So I thought I'd go and visit him. When I arrived at his parents' house I discovered weeds so high in the front garden, and had to push my way through to the front door. Eventually Wilkinson appeared and I went in, to find the place was piled high with newspapers: there must have been several years of them. I don't think he ever went out. It was really very sad. He was neither pleased nor displeased to see me; he just seemed to be in a tunnel. It was extraordinary.

I had another tutor nicknamed Holy Joe, who was a priest, the Rev. Mr Whitehead, a very entertaining man. Some masters admired and liked me, while others detested me. As I was a great reader (fascinated for some time by James Joyce's *Ulysses*), I started to write short stories – and my English master, Mr Lace, said I wrote well enough to go on with it. Looking back, I can see I was inventive, but at the same time my writing was influenced, of course, by my going to the cinema so much. 'In the still of the night, as I gaze from my window, at the moon in its flight, do you love me as I love you.' Another master, Mr Stevenson, when he was in charge of a production of *Lady Precious Stream*, wouldn't have me as an actor, because he decided I was prone to over-act and to play the mimic for laughs. In the end I helped to design the production: 'Pavilion and Banners designed and painted by C. Frankel'.

By December 1939 I had my School Certificate in five subjects – English, Latin, French, Elementary Mathematics and Drawing. To get your matriculation at school you had to have a language as well as mathematics and English, so I went to the polytechnic in Regent's Street, just for a term, and passed the School Certificate in German with flying colours. This was very useful both in the Army and in later life, when I went on to direct films and plays in Germany and Austria. French I learned from the Academy cinema in Oxford Street, where I saw Jean-Louis Barrault in *Les Enfants du Paradis* and *Poile de Carotte* and *Marius* and all those other French films. Nero had given me a basic vocabulary, but my accent and my use of French came entirely from film.

Chapter 3

Oxford 1940–1941

Lillian had said that I should become a barrister, and although my father had always wanted me to have a serious career I didn't take much notice of his advice. I wanted to be a portrait painter or something. My father – he was a remarkable parent – always thought of the best for his children. Because I showed artistic tendencies and a passion for cinema buildings, he put me down for university in New York to study architecture. But I told him I couldn't leave and go off to America when there was a war on.

Although I wouldn't go to America, I thought I might go to university to study Law. When Highgate School was evacuated to Westward Ho! during the war there was just a skeleton staff left in London, and one master, called Mr Twidell, as acting headmaster of what was left: the school had so many buildings in Highgate that they couldn't be totally abandoned. Mr Twidell had been one of my masters, so I went to see him and told him I was thinking of going to Oxford to study Law, and asked how I went about it. He said, 'Go to your father and get a fiver, and go up to Oxford. I suggest you look at Magdalen, which is a lovely college, and you look at St John's, which has great gardens, and you look at Trinity, and possibly Merton. Just go to the college, go along to the lodge, ask if you can speak to the Dean, and see what they say.'

So I went to Oxford, and walked along the High to Magdalen, which I fell in love with – of course, it's so beautiful – and I saw a

14

man called A.J.P. Taylor, a famous philosopher. He said I couldn't possibly start until the next September – and this was, I think, November – what with the war on, and one thing and another. So I visited St John's – and loved walking around the gardens – but got a similar answer. Then I went to Queens: similar answer. Trinity: if there was a possibility it wouldn't be until the new university year – September again.

Finally I went to a smaller college, Oriel, and asked to see the Dean. He wasn't there, but they said I could see the Provost instead. I didn't know what a provost was – I thought it was something to do with the church – but I said all right. So I met Sir David Ross, the Provost, who I discovered was head of the college. When I said I wanted to study there he asked who had recommended me. 'My old housemaster, Mr Twidell.' 'Oh,' he said, 'Twidell. I remember him. He was a pupil of mine. Can you sit for an entrance exam immediately? This evening?' I said I'd have to speak to my father and arrange somewhere to stay. 'Well, six o'clock, come.'

So I rang my father. 'I've been to all these colleges, and this smaller college, Oriel, says I can take an entrance exam this evening, but it can't be any good because everyone else says no.' He said, 'Don't be a bloody fool,' or words to that effect, 'it's a damn good college.' So I found myself a little pub hotel and went back at six in the evening and sat in this huge lecture room, by myself, with examination papers in front of me, and just wrote and wrote, thinking that the more I wrote the better chance I'd have. And then at about half past eight the Provost came in and invited me over to his lodgings. So I did. There I met his wife, Lady Ross, and was offered a glass of cider – I remember in a liqueur glass – and he said, 'We'll let you know.' And I thought, well, that's the end of that. And I went back to London.

To my surprise a few weeks later, around the first week in January a telegram arrived. It said, 'Accepted here. Come immediately.' So off I went, up to Oxford – having missed the first term.

There was no accommodation for me in Oriel itself. During the war many colleges were given over to ministries, and Oriel had the prison commission. So they gave me accommodation in Hertford College – rather nice; it had a Bridge of Sighs – and that's where I met Dom Mintoff, later Prime Minister of Malta, and Peter Carter, who became the Master of Merton, and several other people who became good friends.

The thing about Oxford was the sense of freedom. I couldn't believe it. At school there had been classes and homework and a very regimented life. I went to see my first law tutor, Mr Waldock, and he said, 'I think you should attend this lecture at Trinity on criminal law, this lecture on contracts, a third one here, and, because there's an examination in a year's time – Law Mods – go to the Codrington Library and look up such-and-such books and read chapter one or chapter two . . . and come and see me next week at the same time.' And that was it: I had been given just three one hour lectures a week, and had been asked to go to a library and read a few books. So, despite the fact that it was 1940 and the Germans might arrive at any moment, it was a really happy and relaxed time. I was making friends, rowing, enjoying the pubs . . .

I didn't have a girlfriend to begin with – not until I formed the Ballet Club, when I was immediately enchanted by Anne Cloake; but she turned me down. Then there were Parvati Kumara Mangalum and Joan Royle, and several others. One who became quite a well-known painter was Diana Armfield, whose family I visited in Ringwood. I still have my drawings of them. And Celia. Celia Franca was more than a crush. She was not at Oxford, but was a professional dancer. We talked of marriage. Later she married three times, for a period the dancer Leo Kersley, but she had no children. "Before she passed away, Celia visited London and stayed with Brian Taylor. In discussing her three marriages, she said to Brian, "but I should have married Cyril" - and I agree with her. I showed my appreciation of her in my film "Bold Steps", made for the BBC, but which the BBC has never shown, for some obscure reason.

I thought at Oxford they would know about ballet, but there was nothing. Nevill Coghill, an English lecturer who had translated *The Canterbury Tales* and had founded OUDS (the Oxford University Dramatic Society), was very encouraging when I decided to start a club. Our first venue was the Taylorian, where Sally Gilmore and Walter Gore performed *Confessional*, based on a poem by Browning, and *Bartlemas Fair*: it was jam packed. In the crush afterwards I encountered Hart-Synnot, Bursar at St John's, who told me he thought the venue wasn't suitable. He offered us the facilities of St John's dining hall.

I needed to hire a piano and I needed some music, so I hurried up to the headquarters of the Bach Choir – up in the

Sheldonian, one of these very interesting buildings near All Souls' College. I rushed into the office of Sir Hugh Allen's secretary, a lady called Mrs Molineux, and said, 'I wonder if you can help me, I want to get, er, I want to find, er, a score of, a piece of music called "Jamaican Rumba"' – Arthur Benjamin . . .' She looked at me and said, '*Sit down.* You're running around like a mosquito.' So I sat down. 'Now close your eyes and let the mind be free.' And she left me there for quite some time. Then she said, 'Right, what was it you wanted?' 'I'm sorry I was in a hurry,' I said, 'but I've got to rent a grand piano, and run and do all these things . . .' She replied, 'You sit like that for twenty minutes and it'll be worth at least two hours' sleep in terms of your energy.' This advice had a very powerful effect on me. When I was in the Army, involved in 'action', I was told at two in the afternoon that I'd be going out on night patrol along a river-bed to find out where the Germans were; that sort of thing. Rather than sitting around terrified all afternoon, I simply practised Mrs Molineux's advice.

The Ballet Club was a huge success, mainly because of my London contacts – specifically Marie Rambert. Marie had opened the Ballet Club at the Mercury Theatre in Notting Hill Gate, after Diaghilev died in 1929; there was no Russian Ballet any more. And, Sundays only I think, they trained people like Frederick Ashton and A.V. Coton, a writer who published books on ballet, and Joan Lawson, who became a very good friend and was the sister of Alan Lawson, head of the camera department at ACT, the Film Makers' Union. Members of the Rambert came to Oxford to perform and give talks: great artists like Lydia Sokolova, (who had been the first English ballerina in Diaghilev's Ballets Russes; she was born Hilda Munnings), and Harold Rubin, who ran the Arts Theatre, which did lunchtime ballets. Marie herself came up to Oxford to open our Club, and she was delightful. We took her out on the High and she did cartwheels. We took her into a very smart restaurant and she did cartwheels. It was amazing.

I invited Sally Gilmour (for years Marie's leading dancer) and Walter Gore to come and dance a *divertissement*, and this was one of the most popular events in Oxford. Sally and Walter were the main performers. At this time Walter was creating new ballets, which later went into the Rambert repertoire. Sally, Walter and I had a mutual friend, David Wright, a well-known writer and poet, who was totally deaf. I received a telegram from him one day, saying 'please collect harp from railway station from Sally and Wally'. How did they know I really wanted to play the harp? I had watched these films with Harpo from the Marx Brothers playing the harp, and it was something I would have loved to be able to do. So I went to the railway station, but there was no harp. I went to the Left Luggage: no harp. I thought it was very strange, and when I next spoke to David Wright I said I couldn't find the harp. He couldn't believe I'd really gone to the station. It took me some months to understand that what they were saying was 'You're an angel'. They thought I'd see through their message!

I did a little bit of performing at Oxford, and took ballet classes. I was going to put on a ballet, but Marie Rambert thought we should use professional dancers.

I had two resident pianists, Peter Oldham and Bruce Montgomery (whom I had met initially at Highgate School), and Michael Flanders as a narrator. We staged the first performance in England of *Peter and the Wolf*, with Michael as narrator. Honor Frost, daughter of the Governor of Cyprus, designed the posters and programmes. Her parents were killed in a mountain car crash and she was adopted by their solicitor, Wilfred Evill, who was a great art collector and represented all the unions. Everybody of that period knew of him. Honor became a great friend of my friend Celia, and later they produced a very successful ballet, *Khadza*: Celia did the choreography and Honor produced the design and costumes.

There was an inner excitement to life because of the war. I travelled home occasionally and saw the second Great Fire of London lighting up the night sky, but at Oxford we were apart from it. There was a total optimism that we would win. Apart from my activities with the Ballet Club, I thoroughly enjoyed the lectures, regularly visiting the Codrington Library, a beautiful building, and preparing for the examination.

After you had taken the end of term exam, you went through the main hall and presented yourself to about six of the top lecturers and the Provost. The Provost said, 'I've got a note here from your tutor, Mr Fifoot: "Frankel only came up a few months ago and I don't think there's very much chance of him passing his Moderations."' 'So, how did you get on?' I replied. 'Three distinctions, sir' – and they all more or less applauded. I was very thrilled.

That summer I went on a forestry camp down in Devon, where we cut down trees as part of the war effort. I enjoyed it. Then Honor Frost sent me to *Horizon* magazine: she knew the business manager. *Horizon* was the most important literary magazine in the country at this time, edited by Cyril Connolly and Stephen Spender, and based at offices near Russell Square. The business manager gave me a job at £2 10s a week: I was just the office boy, licking stamps, sealing envelopes, posting letters, buying the cake for tea. Then they discovered he was embezzling the petty cash, so he got the push within a week of my arrival – leaving me as the only person running the office. I climbed in, first thing in the morning, through a compartment you put parcels in, and the phone would ring and it would be Cyril Connolly. And the conversation would go, 'Cyril, this is Cyril.' 'Oh good morning, Cyril, how are you, Cyril?' 'Fine, Cyril. How are you, Cyril?' It used to be marvellous. He'd say to me, 'So what's in the post?' And I might say, 'Well, there's a poem by so-and-so.' 'Oh . . . what's it like?' 'Well, I didn't think much of it.' 'All right, I won't bother to see that.' Suddenly I had power!

At *Horizon*, hanging around, there were Lucien Freud, Louis MacNeice, Augustus John . . . to name just a few. Cyril Connolly didn't like younger people usually, but he had a gorgeous ladyfriend called Lys Lubbock, who was married to an actor, Ian Lubbock. He preferred boys to girls, and was the son of the headmaster of Eton – which is probably why he preferred boys. So Lys became Cyril's mistress, and eventually changed her name by deed poll to Connolly. She and I got on like a house on fire, and partly because of that Cyril Connolly was very nice to me. When I was going off into the Army he arranged a lunch for me at the White Tower restaurant in Percy Street, which was splendid, and while I was in the Army he sent me, wherever I was in the world, a copy of *Horizon* . . . until we had broken out of Cassino and had got to the Anzio beachhead below Rome. When my *Horizon* arrived there was an editorial by Connolly saying that the worst thing that could happen was damage to the monastery at Cassino. I wrote to him to say that I thought the life of one person was more valuable than all the bricks. *Horizon* stopped arriving, and he never spoke to me again.

At Oxford I had a friend with a long wave radio, which was rare in those days. It could receive programmes from all round the world. On one occasion I was with him and heard this screaming match going on. It was Hitler giving a speech. My schoolboy German was good enough for me to realise that this man was a lunatic.

I wanted to volunteer for the Air Force, but because of my age my father had to sign my application and he wouldn't. So I volunteered for the Army: I would have been called up anyway at eighteen. And so in 1941, after less than a year, I left Oxford for the first time.

Chapter 4

Army 1941–1946

began in the Army, early in the autumn, as a trooper in the RAC, the Royal Armoured Corps. I went to various camps, what they called schemes in those days, and I learnt about armoured cars. As soon as I could I applied for a commission: better conditions, and a better uniform. I didn't have my degree, only my moderations – so they would judge me purely as a military person. I went in front of a board of six people. I'd had a fall out of a tank and had my arm in a sling. The one at the end, whom I gauged to be the psychiatrist, leant forward and said, 'You're not really mechanically minded, are you?' Despite this, I was convincing enough to scrape through to Sandhurst. By December I was there, and, like Oxford, I was there for less than a year.

By this time I didn't view myself as of any religion. I'd been reading Aldous Huxley and his *The Perennial Philosophy*. I wasn't aware of any anti-semitism.

At Sandhurst I became friendly with a man called Michael Frostick, later a prolific motoring writer and behind a popular car series for the BBC. He and his wife died tragically in a car in Denmark in the 1960s. He and I discovered a disused and dilapidated theatre. There were no entertainments at Sandhurst, so we decided, with the help of a lieutenant, John Gray, one of the instructors, to doll it up. The first thing we did was a show called *Divertissement*, which was based on all my ballet experiences. It was just silhouette, colour and shadow to music.

And it was quite successful. It was full of different things. In one sketch I remember that John Gray went on with a piece of newspaper, and mimed eating hot chips to a piece of music by Stravinsky. I did something in silhouette from a *Symphony Fantastique* movement where a man is being hanged: there was the noose and I was swinging.

While I was at Sandhurst I went up to London to visit the new London Film Society (which later became the British Film Institute), where I met a lady called Olwen Vaughan, who later founded the National Film Institute. Through her I booked a French film called *Poil de Carotte*, the Marcel Pagnol trilogy *Marius*, *Fanny* and *Cesar*) and several other important French films to show to the cadets. They went down well. I also put on concerts of music and then CEMA, the equivalent of the Arts Council, offered me a production of *Man With a Load of Mischief* by Ashley Dukes, Marie Rambert's husband, who owned the Mercury Theatre.

My parents came to the passing-out parade. Michael Frostick was going to join the First Royal Dragoons, but they had no more spaces available. I decided to go for the King's Dragoon Guards. They had a lovely double headed eagle as a badge, which I found appealing. I met a former colonel of theirs, called Howes, who seemed to like me and put me forward. But it was some months before I was sent abroad to join the regiment in North Africa.

It was after my twenty-first birthday – for which my parents threw me a party at the Hyde Park Hotel – that I went up to Liverpool and boarded a boat that was heading for Algiers. On the journey I met the Brooke brothers, sons of the politician Lord Allan Brooke, and Rachel Cunningham, the daughter of Admiral Cunningham. We had a fun time. The ship was fantastic, because, as I'm sure you know, rationing was very strict in England during the war. Having travelled overnight to Liverpool, and boarded the boat at breakfast time, I remember the thrill of the long lists on the menu the waiter gave me: everything you could ever want for breakfast. I said I didn't know what to choose, so the waiter suggested I should have everything. It was a civilian liner that had been requisitioned by the Army as troop transport, and the same waiting staff had been kept on. But for the fear of being sunk by a U-boat, it was a jolly trip.

In Algiers the fun continued, to begin with. We enjoyed ourselves, renting a motor launch, playing card games and finding little restaurants. It was a happy period. The King's Dragoon Guards were not based in Algiers but much further into the desert in Tunisia, near Tripoli. When, eventually, I went by truck to join them the fun stopped. I developed dysentery, which was dreadful: I don't think I've ever been so ill since. I had a temperature of 105 and took something like twenty-six sulphur grenadine tablets. Absolutely awful. Anyhow, when I finally recovered a car came to take me to the regiment. I met the Colonel, Hermon his name was, and he was charming: he came from the Royal Dragoons but was now Lieutenant-Colonel in charge of the King's Dragoon Guards. And he sent me to C squadron or D squadron, I think it was.

By the time I got to the squadron it was evening, I remember – and this chap Selby, who was the squadron leader, took one look at me and turned to someone and said, 'What's Puggy Howes up to sending us people like this?' This was just from looking at me. And then someone said, 'Are you good on a horse?' I replied that I'd actually never ridden a horse. 'Good Lord, he's never ridden a horse!' It was only this major, Lord Selby, and one or two others who made me feel unwelcome. I visited a number of squadrons and messes, did my imitations of Churchill, and others, and brought the house down. But as we went on into war in Italy I found – or my batman found – that I was the one who was being given all the dangerous patrols. I came back from one promptly, having got my information, correct or otherwise, and saw the major's face fall on seeing me. I realised that he was trying to get me bumped off; so I asked for a transfer. It was a very unhappy period for me.

Many years later my father, a bridge player, was a member of the Hamilton Club off Park Lane. In conversation with a fellow member who had been a squadron leader of the King's Dragoon Guards, he was told, 'We had a Jew boy who got up to no good'. My father promptly resigned from the club.

Things changed when I was transferred to the 5th Reconnaissance Regiment, doing precisely the same reconnaissance job in similar armoured vehicles. Arthur Prince was my squadron leader there. I walked into his squadron, and was told he wasn't there. When I asked when he'd be back they said, 'We don't know. He's gone to the Naples Opera.' I knew then that I was in the right place. The opera continued in Italy during the war. It was like going to the music hall in England. Everybody went informally, taking oranges and peeling and eating them during the arias. The Italians knew all the tunes and the words and joined in!

While taking a reconnaissance course outside Salerno, I rounded up a lot of people and said, 'Let's go to the opera.' So we got to the opera and it had already started. The commissionaire said, 'No, no, no, impossiblay,' to which I replied, 'No, no, no, it *is* possible, we stand at the back.' Anyhow, we pushed past and got in – just in time to see someone on the stage sing 'Aha-aaa!' and the curtain came down. But we went to a nice restaurant and had delicious Marsala.

On the course in Salerno there was this chap called Charlie Newton, who with another guy was always taking the mickey out of everybody, so I was rather on guard. But on one occasion I wanted to go to Naples to go to the opera and he offered me a lift. And it was totally different. It was a really loving person whom I was speaking to, and I really felt in accord with him. But the course finished, and as he was in the Green Howards and I was in the Reconnaissance Regiment we were not in direct touch. But when we made the breakthrough from Anzio to Rome, in the hills just outside Anzio I came across his grave. Raleigh Trevelyan, who was also in the Green Howards, wrote a book about Anzio (*The Fortress*), which was dedicated to him.

The 5th Reconnaissance were the first in Naples. I was on the newsreels. The Germans were moving back up to the river Arno, and we were sent ahead into the city to check the lay of the land before the ground troops moved in. I was in a little scout car, exploring up near the Fiumicino airport, when suddenly I saw the silhouette of a Tiger tank coming towards me. It fired at me, but the scout car was only about so high and the shell went over my head. I said, 'Into reverse!' and we scrambled back.

On another occasion, just north of Naples, I came up to a canal – again in a scout car. I approached round the side of a building, and suddenly realised that on the other side of the canal there was a man in strange uniform. He was looking at me and I was looking at him. Then he realised I was British and I realised he was German, and we both fled. But within minutes a sniper was firing at us, and the man in front of me was hit. I had to get him into the back of my scout car and rush him to hospital, which was some miles away – but the Italians in their characteristic way were going mad, because the British were there and the *Tedeschi*, the Germans, were being got rid of, and they pelted us with flowers and fruit. The custard apples were hard, like cricket balls, and I was saying, 'No, no,' because they were hitting this poor man lying in the back of the car.

I was never fond of Naples. I didn't really have a good experience there. It's a difficult place at the best of times. Things got better when we moved north, into the dug-outs in Anzio. We were stuck for the winter outside Cassino, and it rained. We were in bivouac tents, and I remember floating.

I've talked about Mrs Molineux's advice. When the time came to go out on night patrol, and it was just me and the sergeant, I felt completely in control. Absolutely. I knew what to do. One evening we went along the river bed, and after going along 100 yards suddenly there was a scramble in front of us – and it was a dog. So we continued, and after about 400 yards we were fired on from five different positions – and these bullets were literally skimming past my face. I said to Sergeant Ferguson, 'Stay there,' and listened. I could hear them loading a mortar on the other side of the river bed, and they fired one which didn't come near us. Then I heard them beginning to reload it and I knew exactly how many seconds it would take, so I said to the sergeant, 'Up there and *run*.' I followed him – and we came back. He was in a state of shock, but I remained cool, calm and collected, as they say – thanks to Mrs Molineux and that advice in Oxford, 'Close your eyes'.

The Germans continued to retreat, and by the summer we were entering Rome. There were all these beautifully dressed women: they were nearly all in white, and they nearly all had a black patent leather belt and maybe a red scarf. All the hotels were operating. Rome was operating. It was quite bewildering and breathtaking.

By this stage in the war there was no opportunity for leave back in England – and I didn't return there until the war was over. Once the situation in Italy had settled, before we went to southern France, the 5th Reconnaissance Regiment boated over to Palestine. We were to be a kind of military police force. The Arabs wanted the Jews out, and everyone wanted the British out: we were stuck in the middle. At night Arabs came crawling on the sand into our camp to pinch guns, or whatever they could get. Meanwhile the Stern Gang, as they were called – Jewish extremists – were blowing up bridges. There was the famous bombing of King David's Hotel in Jerusalem.

I was lucky, again. Although to begin with I had been disenchanted by Tel Aviv, one evening I went to a dance performance given by the Palestine Folk Opera, and it was wonderful, especially the choreography, by a woman called Gertrude Kraus. I sought her out and said I would like a lesson from her, and we became very close friends. Gertrude was a very very gifted artist, not only a dancer and choreographer but a sculptress, painter and chess player. She introduced me to the nightlife, the real life behind this commercial city's façade, and I went to chess clubs and coffee houses. What was interesting was seeing men who worked in the city, road workers and so on, stopping for their lunch break, sitting on the pavement and perhaps bringing out a violin. They were highly civilised people who just happened to be doing manual jobs.

In the bookshops in Tel Aviv they had a lot of books from Russia. There was one particular volume, surprisingly translated into English, on mime – and for me it became almost a Bible. My knowledge of dance, and mime in dance, made me conscious of these two art forms wherever I went. And when I found anyone who taught dance or mime I asked them to give me a lesson.

From Palestine we came back to France for the crossing of the Elbe, which was the last stage of the war. I also spent a little bit of time in Flemish Belgium, in a small village called Zaffalaere. I was billeted with a very friendly family. This was where I first encountered a V-bomb, which scared me. The V-bomb is the one where there was a noise which cut out into sudden silence, then dropped and exploded. The good thing about this place was that my cousin Gerald, whom I'd been brought up with, was nearby in Ghent, so I was able to link up with him.

Then we were off across Germany. I was shocked when we drove through the north of the country to see the damage: whole towns had been wiped out.

Colonel Douglas Pennant, a very charming, quiet chap, and I were in an armoured car exploring the plain at Flensberg near the Baltic when we came to this town Neustadt, north of Lübeck, where there were people running around in striped pyjamas. It took a few moments for us to realise they were concentration camp prisoners. Hitler and Himmler were moving these prisoners north, because the British had crossed the Elbe and were advancing and they didn't want the evidence: they wanted to shove them out to Norway or somewhere. One boat had already left, but there were still thousands. Of course nobody in the town knew what was going on – or so they said. When we took the mayor around and showed him, and told him to go and organise food and this, that and the other, he ran away. He wasn't there the next morning. If you spoke to any German they'd say, 'Oh no, they're all criminals, they're all criminals.' And if you said, 'Are you a member of the Nazi party?' 'Oh no . . .' but we knew he was.

I was led into this great hangar where there were thousands of prisoners. I stood on a box and, because I spoke German, explained that the British had arrived and that we would provide them with food and medicine and their worries were over. My little speech was greeted by silence. And then in the distance started this thin cheer, which grew and grew and grew and absolutely overcame me. Then we went and saw what was outside the hangar: these smashed bodies, tied together and bashed about. I can't – I don't like talking about it. The next morning I gave the instructions for everyone to come out onto the grass outside. I think there must have been something like 1200 bodies left inside.

That evening when we got back to where we were staying, Travemünde, we were in the Mess, having a drink, and over the radio came the news that the war was over. And nobody reacted. One by one we got up and went to bed. We'd had such shocking experiences in this concentration camp, I can't tell you. When you see battered bodies and brains on the floor . . . Then typhus broke out . . .

I had one young chap who could speak some English going round with me and he was very helpful. Every nationality was there. There were Dutch Jews, Jews from Poland, Czechoslovakia, Germany, France, Italy . . . DPs they were called. Displaced People.

With the war over, a Field Marshal Erhardt Milch turned up to surrender to me. But he wanted to be dealt with by someone of an equivalent rank – because I was then only a captain – and so I got in touch with Headquarters. Brigadier Derek Mills Roberts turned up, took the Field Marshal's baton, said, 'You're a war criminal', and bashed him with it until he broke it! Milch was dragged off and sentenced in Nuremberg by the prosecutor Sir Hartley Shawcross.

After some months of organising DPs I was invited to go to Divisional Level in charge of Army Welfare Services in Brunswick:

I had been providing entertainments and was a natural choice. It was from there that I had the opportunity to help run four opera houses, and stage innumerable revues and plays that toured the British Zone.

Brunswick had suffered bomb damage, but the townsfolk demonstrated, wanting their opera house to be restored before homes. As a result the opera house was soon producing *Madame Butterfly*, *Hansel und Gretel* and regular orchestral concerts, under the guidance of conductor Artur Bittner. My colleague in Brunswick was Brian Taylor, who had a passion for music and theatre. We decided to arrange a series of performances based at the theatre in nearby Wolfenbutel, and these were very popular. Brian, who had previously worked in Berlin, urged me to meet the conductor of the Berlin Philharmonic, Sergiu Celibidache, and I agreed to travel with him to Berlin.

Over the border, in the Russian Zone, we visited a place called Völkenrode, which is where they had originally made the Volkswagen; now it was an experimental scientific place. The V-bomb among other things had been developed there. It was full of amazing things. There was one machine surrounded by nylon curtains (they had invented nylon) and it was at least the size of a room. When they pulled the curtains open there were all these cogs and chains, and I asked the chap who was supervising this semi-museum what it was invented for. 'Oh,' he replied, 'this was invented to make the perfect point to a lead pencil.' This for me symbolised the distinction between the German mind and the British mind: we would just use a razor blade.

I was enthralled by Celibidache and was able to persuade him to perform for us with his orchestra in Wolfenbutel. Brian had previously worked in Hanover as well as Berlin and so we were also able to bring in concerts by the Hanover Symphony Orchestra and the Hanover State Opera, both live and for broadcast. It was an exciting period.

I was running all these entertainments, operas, orchestras and even a circus, for something like eighteen months. This is where I met many lifelong friends, like Brian Taylor, and others whom I was to work with in later life, like Richard Stone and Ian Carmichael. I was in 5 Division, but Richard Stone and I were Army Welfare Services at Corps level – which embraced three or four divisions that made up all the British Forces in Germany. Once a month, or so, I went to Corps HQ, which was in another town, and they'd ask what I had for them. And I'd reply, 'What have you got for me?' They mainly worked with ENSA, which provided shows on tour from England. The American equivalent was the VSO, which sent Bob Hope around the world.

I remember putting on a play called *Elizabeth*, about Queen Elizabeth, with a great actress called Beatrice Lehmann. I shall never forget being backstage when she was about to go on. She said, 'Huup! – I've got hiccups!' and I more or less had to push her on stage. She didn't hiccup once during her scene – and when she came off stage she immediately started hiccupping again. We had a great laugh about that.

In Brunswick there was not only a very good Salvation Army canteen for the Forces, there was also a JHC (Jewish Hospitality Committee) canteen, run by a man called Ben Toff. Ben became one of my best friends; he was a wonderful character. His father had been a horse-drawn cab driver, and his brother was not only a taxi driver but ran the taxi drivers' magazine as well. They were a lovely family; they lived just by Kingsway, Holborn.

Brian, like me, became a close friend of Ben Toff. When he returned to civilian life Brian continued to produce plays and musical events – in particular a play called *Uncle Harry* – with Ben. Brian was planning to become a teacher, but I encouraged him to think about entering the entertainment world. He took my advice, and on leaving the Army he joined the Film Division of the Ministry of Information, where he encountered John Grierson and was later put in charge of Danziger Film Studios in Borehamwood. Later he produced a highly popular television show called *Cool for Cats*. The association with the Danzigers continued, and he created the Mayfair Theatre.

General Gregson-Ellis took a box for the Celibidache concert. As I remember, it was he who recommended me when an opportunity to move to Corps level arose. That's when I got my promotion. The chap who was Director of Army Welfare Services was demobbed and the post, which was a major's post, became vacant. I was possibly the youngest major in the Army.

At one point I managed to get on a military aircraft to Paris to see Celia, who was performing with the Sadler's Wells Ballet (later the Royal Ballet). It was wonderful to see her again and catch up with news about old friends from Oxford. And in Paris there was food the like of which we'd not seen in years.

I spent time on the border with the Russians. As an intelligence officer I got to know some of the Russians, despite the 'non-fraternisation' we were meant to be practising. We exchanged belts, and they gave me a photograph which they had signed on the back.

I had very strong feelings about the Germans, as you can imagine, but every now and again I met an artist. One such is Ferry Gebhardt, who was a very fine pianist and a warm human being whom we brought down from Hamburg to play in Brunswick and elsewhere.

One particularly special relationship was with an Austrian circus. Two gentlemen who represented the Circus Barum waited several hours outside my office to meet me. From childhood onwards I have been enthralled and excited by circuses – Bertram Mills in particular – so when these chaps told me their circus was assembling at Einbeck the following Monday, and that it would be worth my while to see it, I went. I met the owner and his daughter Margaretta when they were waiting for the band, which never did arrive. So rehearsals began, with Margaretta leading a troupe of horses that danced with entertaining footwork without the music. The owner talked at length of their needs, including food, particularly for the animals – horses, dogs and Tony the young elephant. They also had a lion, but he was unwell because they couldn't get sufficient meat for him – and unfortunately neither could I. Anyway, I went to see Gregson-Ellis and arranged to provide the circus with accommodation and army rations. Over the next month I was repeatedly put under arrest by the Military Police for doing this – but as I had the General's blessing these charges were never followed through.

They came to see me again when storms tore their big top. I had to think hard. Finally I went to the Army Stationery Office and acquired about twenty small jars of Seccotine; then I met them near Hanover, where we spent hours sticking their tent back together.

I arranged that Army personnel could attend performances for a small fee, which every quarter would be paid to my office. I recall how they did arrive on one occasion with a huge amount of cash, which was used to establish a rest centre in Bad Salzberg, south of Brunswick.

The circus performances were full of excitement. Tony the elephant would gently, step by step, walk along an upturned plank, and there were clowns and acrobats galore as well as the wonderful dancing horses.

When, finally, the sad occasion came for me to bid them farewell, Brian, Ben and I attended a performance where each act bowed to me. I was astounded at the improved condition of the seating and refreshments, and when I was invited into one of the caravans, which previously had been tawdry, but were now luxurious and decorated superbly, I asked how they had achieved this. They said, 'Don't you remember? You signed for permission for us to buy stuff from the Army salvage dumps.'

Many years later, when making a film in Germany, I saw posters for Circus Barum and attended a performance. It was nothing like as exciting as it had been. I went backstage and discovered it was no longer run by the same family. In some ways this was a disappointment, but it increased my appreciation of what they had been.

Around this time I received a letter from one of the old gang from the Sherwood Foresters Regiment days: we knew him as 'Petal'. He was now at the Inns of Court Regiment, somewhere or other.

> Dear Old Frankie [I was known as Frankie],
> Can't remember how long it is since I heard from you. So it's finished and we're both out alive. How? I'm sure I don't know. My worst and closest was bumping into a nest of five, yes five, 88s [that's tanks with guns] – and they all missed me! though one's shell took my aerial away, one foot above the turret. Hey ho, that's just one incident out of far too many. I should imagine you had more than me because you've had it longer. Think you've got the best of it, old lad. Filled with envy too to hear of your various leaves in all those romantic, trendy spots and now you've got all those lovely Italians to play with. For us we can't have a bash at the German girls even if we should want to. It's hard, but certainly necessary. No sign of much possible warfare here. We're fairly rounding up SS, Gestapo and other undesirable square-heads and without much trouble either. I've taken over the job of unit education officer and why am I volunteering for all this work whilst others

are doing not much? 'Cos I see a big chance of getting a third star back again. Most essential. Peter Mosley is a captain in the Belgium Armoured Car Regiment. Jilly was a Troup Commander in the F&F tanks and I constantly met him all through the action. Hell, I'm crazy, of course you're over here now but where the hell I don't know. What shall I do? I'll have to send this on trial to you care of British Land Forces (you know BLF). Howard Wayley I also saw in the thick of an action, airborne type you know. Cheers cock. I've just come back from England Leave. My oh my.

Ever, Petal.

Chapter 5

Back to Oxford 1946–1947

Having survived the war, by good fortune, I returned to Oxford to complete my degree.

Some things had not changed. I remember through Baroness Ravensdale, daughter of Lord Curzon, I was introduced to Lady Cunard, who said to me, while I was still in uniform, 'Where have you come from? . . . Did you meet Hitler? I met him in Berchtesgaden in 1938. Fascinating chap.'

I didn't run the Ballet Club in my second Oxford period. After I left for the Army in 1941 the people who'd been associated with me carried on with it for a bit, then others took over. It was still going when I came back in '47, but I chose not to get involved.

I joined the Newlands Society at Oriel College, which was a play-reading society run by the Dean: we gathered on a Wednesday evening and read a play, and once a year put on a play. When they were discussing what to produce I said I wanted to do *L'Enfant Prodigue*. I had seen a production of it at the Mercury Theatre with a very good cast, including Celia and a wonderful actor called Alan Badel as the lead. He died young, and was, in my opinion, one of the finest actors of the twentieth century. In the Newlands production, which I directed, the lead was played by Sandy Wilson, an undergraduate at Oriel. It was a huge success, and I enjoyed it enormously. Sandy wrote in his autobiography, *I Could Be Happy* (1975):

I think that in many ways it was one of the most extraordinary experiences of my life. By sheer force of personality Cyril turned us, in a matter of weeks, into accomplished pantomimists, and in a role which kept me on stage almost throughout the play I was able to acquit myself with distinction, something that I have never done again from that day to this and which still continues to astonish me.

Sandy later wove the Pierrot Pierrette theme into his international hit, *The Boyfriend.*

Everything was more relaxed at Oxford after the war. It was a happy time. When I finally earned my degree I had to decide what career course to follow. Should I be a portrait painter? An architect? My parents put pressure on me to study for an MA in law, but I was keen to get work in the entertainment world. Nevill Coghill, the English don who had founded OUDS, wrote to me that summer:

> Dear Cyril,
> Your letter came just when you were in my thoughts. I've just written to Professor Westrup to suggest you as the producer for next term's Opera Club performance of *Il Domineo* and now I learn from you that you are thinking of going down. Well, if you have a positive entry into the professional world you'd be wise to take it. But if not, as appears from your letter, I should think twice . . . As you say lots of people ask me how to get on to the professional stage. I always answer, I don't know. And that's the truth. It's bad enough for an actor, but for a producer it's out of the question except by fluke. I couldn't get a job as a producer myself as far as I know. Thank goodness I'm not trying. And so can still less help you, except by sympathy. The only way is to get yourself known. Peter Brook did so by making a film and showing it to everybody. At last the Chante Clair people

said, come and produce for us, and he has
made a success at that. And then was asked
to Stratford. And now is a star. All is fortune,
as Malvolio says. It might help to produce *Il
Domineo* . . . Do you know all the people at
Covent Garden? If not you might go and see
Patrick Terry, as a friend of mine. You will be
sure of kindness and friendliness from him.
But he could hardly be able to help more than
by telling you the general set up. He is very
interested in Ballet and has something to do
with the organisation there. I'm not sure
what, but he's the only person I know well
enough to approach on your behalf. He is
about your age. No one could help liking him.
He is also lively and intelligent and not one of
the self-seeking crook kind that haunt the
theatre.
Best wishes, Nevill Coghill. 28th August 1947.

So I went to see this guy Patrick Terry, and he arranged a
meeting with the head of Covent Garden, who was called Webster
– known as 'Piggy' Webster because he was fat and round. I told
him I wanted to direct opera and he told me he might be able to
find a place for me in the press department. Then I met the press
people, and they more or less said I could have a job with them,
but I didn't want that. So I rang up my friend Michael Frostick,
whom I knew needed a job very much as he'd just married: his
wife was a Danish dancer, Osa Bonda. And he got the job. This
was marvellous for me because it meant that every time I went to
the opera or the ballet I was in the press box!

Then my friend Kay Ambrose offered me a job. Kay, a
wonderful illustrator and writer about ballet, had lectured for me
at Oxford, and I was a frequent visitor to her home on Kew
Green; Celia Franca had moved to live with her. Kay had become
very close to the great Indian dancer of the time, Ram Gopal, who
was giving performances at one of the West End theatres – I
think it was the Saville – and Kay asked if I would stage manage
or stage direct. But again this was not what I wanted to do, so I
sent Ben Toff, who had been stage director for Billy Cotton's
band and several shows at the Palladium before the war. Off he

went to stage-manage Ram Gopal, and then a Spanish dancer called Esmerelda. These shows were impresarioed by a wonderful man called Julian Brunsweg, who was only about 4ft 6in, and a bit round. His wife, Vera, had been in a concentration camp. If the phone rang he'd pick it up and say, 'Who am I?'. His English was very funny. He was terrific at setting things up, and got Anton Dolin and Alicia Markova to tour with Grace Cone's School of Dancers round England. Dolin had been a Diaghilev dancer, and was the one English, or Irish, dancer (his real name was Patrick Anton) to team up with Markova. Cone's pupils became the Corps De Ballet, and with the two stars they put on a performance initially at the Albert Hall, I think; it later found a home in the Stoll Theatre. Markova and I became very friendly over this period.

Later on, during the Festival of Britain in 1951, Ben, who by then was second in command of Brunsweg's company, built a proscenium theatre with scaffolding in the Festival Hall. I suggested it be called the Festival Ballet; it is now the English National Ballet. In the same way that there isn't a theatre named after Lilian Baylis, who founded the Old Vic, which led to the founding of the National Theatre and to the founding of the Sadler's Wells Ballet, there is no memorial to Julian Brunsweg. There's a bronze bust of Henry Wood, who founded the Promenade concerts, but most people who found these important cultural showpieces somehow get forgotten.

Back in 1947 I became responsible for doing all their publicity, press hand-outs and one thing or another. But it was film or theatre that I wanted to pursue. I tried to get a position in the film industry but immediately came up against the union. You couldn't work in the industry unless you were in the union, and you couldn't be in the union until you were working in the industry.

When I ran the Ballet Club I'd worked with Joan Lawson, who had been a dancer and had spent time in Russia; she lived not far from where my parents lived in Hampstead Garden Suburb. I went to visit her and discovered that her father had been one of the founder members of the Film Union – he gave me a book called *The Literature of Film* – and her brother was Alan Lawson, who became head of the cameramen's section of the Union.

I wrote to Mr Craig at the ACT, but his answer was a flat no. Then I wrote to John Wolff at GDF Film Distributors Ltd. He replied on 22 August 1947: 'Dear Major Frankel, thank you for your letter of the 21st. I should be pleased to see you here Tuesday next at 12 o'clock if convenient to you.' At that meeting he suggested I should meet Michael Balcon of Ealing Studios. On 22 September Woolf wrote again:

> Dear Mr Frankel,
> Many thanks for your letter, I'm extremely pleased to hear that Mr Balcon is going to try and fit you into his organisation and I'm sure that if and when he does you will make a great success. You have my very best wishes.
> Yours sincerely, John Woolf

When I met Michael Balcon he said that I should talk to Stella Joncleere, who was in charge of his literary department. She said that they could possibly give me a job reading scripts, but I wanted to get into active production.

I finally decided that I had to confront the Union. I made my way to Soho Square and asked to meet Mr Craig. He continued to say no, but I continued not to leave. Finally I lent forward and said that there must be a loophole. After a time he lifted his head and whispered, 'Laboratories'.

I hurried to the public library and looked in the *Annual Film Industry Survey* under 'Laboratories'. There were several, including one owned by John Woolf, so I went back to him. He picked up the phone and made an appointment for me with its director. And so I was given a job at GDF Film Laboratories at Lime Grove Film Studios. On my first day I sat there all morning watching the machines. At my lunchbreak I went out to get a sandwich and walked straight into my old school chum Alvin Bailey, with a very attractive lady, Anne Coates: they were both film editors there. At last I felt I was in the film industry.

In November I received another letter from Michael Balcon:

> I'm delighted to have your letter of 10th November. By joining the Film Industry through the laboratory side you have taken a most admirable step. In point of fact all of the people I have met who have had a terrific urge to get into film production have managed to get in somehow and most of them have ended up with prospects of a good and lasting

career. In any case, the basic experience you gain will be invaluable to you I'm sure.

And so I got my membership card: '1946/8 – Newcomer – GDF Lab Shepherds Bush.'

But how to get over to production? When I read that the Rank Organisation was setting up Highbury Studios, in order to encourage new talent, I went along and offered myself as an assistant director. Although two unsuitable candidates had already been sent home, there was still a reluctance from the shop steward to accept me. When I told my friends at the labs they more or less threatened to go on strike if I wasn't allowed to move into production.

And so I managed to get a job as third assistant on *Passport to Pimlico*.

Chapter 6

Crown Film Unit & Group 3 1947–1953

To my surprise Highbury Studios failed. Soon everybody there was looking for work. By chance, another assistant director told me of an interview he had had at Crown Film, but that all they wanted was a 'chief cook and bottlewasher' and he wasn't interested. On *Passport to Pimlico* my duties had been getting the first assistant his sandwiches and controlling traffic, so 'chief cook and bottlewasher' appealed to me. When I contacted Henry Geddes at Crown he offered me a job on £7 a week, which just about paid my travel to and from Beaconsfield.

My first full assignment at Crown was as an assistant director to the lady director Di Pine. We flew to New York to make the documentary *Wonder Jet*, tracking the influence of British technology around the world. We flew British Airways; the hostesses helped us out with some currency and we got rooms at the same hotel as them, the Roosevelt. The head of cabin crew invited us for a drink at the top of the Rockefeller Center.

I directed my very first shot in Bristol, where they were building the Brabazon aeroplane: one of the ministries wanted some coverage. The Brabazon was enormous, and I had to get a shot of these hangar doors opening. I was terribly nervous. I had a cameraman with me who was a real veteran, Jonah Jones, and when he sensed I was nervous he kept telling funny stories, kept talking all the time. Anyhow, we did it.

I went on to direct a number of documentaries myself – *Explorers of the Depths, Welcome To Our Table, Auto Suggestion, World of Books, Wing to Wing.* It was *Explorers of the Depths* that brought me to John Grierson's attention. I did a report on trawling, mainly about over-fishing, and then made this film, the subject of which remains topical today. Grierson had brought over a brilliant producer of *World in Action* in Canada, Stuart Legg, to do *World in Action* in Britain. He wrote to me about *Explorers*: 'The Scottish Home Department warmly approved the Torry research film at the rough cut stage, making only a few amendments. It is a first rate piece of work. I believe that there's enough material for a longer two-reel version . . .'

On 15 March 1951 the *Listener* wrote:

> There was a short film deserving mention, a
> Crown Film production called *Explorers of the
> Depths* which took us on a trip in trawler
> fitted out to study life on or near the floor of
> the North Sea. The film records the ingenious
> and surprising efforts now being made to
> solve the mystery of fish supply changes and
> shortages. Not an entrancing subject you may
> think if you missed it. Speaking for oneself
> and remembering the very good photography
> one is glad not to have missed it.

On the film, I used Jimmy Hodges, the Admiralty's underwater cameraman. When the Russians brought a destroyer into the Channel the Admiralty sent him down with a camera to see whether there was anything funny going on – and he vanished. He was lovely to work with.

When I first went up to Scotland to discuss the film I met a man called Forsyth Hardy in Edinburgh; he was later a biographer of Grierson but at that time was head of the film department of the Scottish Office. When I arrived there were two or three people in his office apart from himself. They ordered coffee, but not for me. Then at a quarter to one they said, 'It's lunchtime. See you back here at quarter past two.' That was my introduction to Scottish hospitality.

When I got up to the north-east corner of Scotland, planning to go on a trawler, I went to the office of this man called Lucas, who was in charge of the fisheries for the state. I said I wanted to go out in a trawler, and I wanted to do this and I wanted to do that, and he said that it could be arranged. Then I said, 'I'm staying at the Ship Hotel. Can I invite you for a drink?' 'I beg your pardon?' 'I said I'm staying at the hotel, and can I invite you for a drink?' 'Would you say that again?' 'I'm just down the road at the hotel and I wondered if I could invite you for a drink.' He said, 'I've been here three years and that's the first time anybody's invited me for a drink – I'd love to!'

The next film I made was less well received. *Welcome To Our Table* prompted questions to be asked in Parliament: how could a Government Film Unit make a film about British food when we had rationing? Among the foods we celebrated were Oxford marmalade, with Mr Frank Cooper himself, kippers and Stilton cheese. You assume Stilton comes from Stilton, but it doesn't: it's produced with milk from the cows that graze in Rutland, the smallest county, in the middle of England. The farmer who first produced it had a brother who ran a horse and coach ride from London going up north, and one of their first stops was at a pub in the village of Stilton. He sent his cheese to this one pub, and that's how it got its name. Drambuie, with its recipe from Bonnie Prince Charlie, was also included. I met the Drambuie family, and was invited to their home and I cannot tell you the hospitality I received. They were the exception to my experience of Scottish hospitality.

The last job I did for Crown was one that I had proposed: 1952's *The Nutcracker – Pas De Deux*, was a ballet film with Belinda Wright and John Gilpin. Having the relationship with Festival Ballet, I welcomed the opportunity to marry camera technique with choreography. Later, when I was away in Africa, I received this note from John Baxtor at Group 3 (which was funded by the National Film Finance Corporation), dated 12 December 1952:

> Dear Cyril
> . . . let me tell you about the Ballet short. Mr Lawrie [John Lawrie, Chairman of Group 3] was enchanted. Sir Michael [Balcon: Group 3's chairman] praised the dancing, music and direction. He was non-committal about the colour. Perhaps because he is working making a Technicolor picture. When Mr Lawrie saw the picture, he brought some

> members of the staff. They all liked it very
> much. I have promised to show it Ben Toff
> next week . . .

When Ben had seen the film he telegrammed me himself: 'I have just seen *Nutcracker.* I agree absolute triumph for you. First real ballet film.'

Man of Africa, 1953

I first went to Africa not to make *Man of Africa* but to make a feature-length documentary for the Colonial Office. I went on my own and just talked to people; I was particularly keen to meet what we would call the 'pagan' people – by 'pagans' I mean they had not yet been influenced by either Catholic or Protestant missionaries. I was going to places where the people had never seen a white man before. And when I got on a plane to go to Uganda, which was going to take twenty-three hours – a flying boat, which was going to land on Lake Victoria – I was sitting there thinking, my God, I've never seen a black man, how will I recognise one from another? Because in London then there weren't any. It was extraordinary.

After travelling many miles through the countryside of Uganda I found a group – more a family than a tribe – who entertained me with dancing and singing, then decided it was time to have something to eat. They all sat down and had some food which had been cooked over a log fire; but I didn't get any. I said that I'd like some food, and they said, 'Didn't you bring some with you?' And I said that I hadn't. 'You mean you would eat our food?' 'Of course.' And so they brought me some roasted corn and some fruits, and then went back to their singing and dancing. I felt I had to contribute, so I joined in the dance. This produced such peals of laughter, but I enjoyed it. Then I was presented with chickens and honey, and for one moment thought I was going to be presented with a wife.

The pagans were not monogamous. A man's wealth was judged by how many wives he had. A wife could be bought with two cows and five goats, which was quite something. Each wife had a hut, all next door to each other, and the first was the senior wife. The husband spent a night, shall we say, with each in turn, which created harmony. Once the missionaries got hold of these people and they were only allowed one wife the whole social structure was upset. It was the women who worked in the fields and the men who marketed. I remember, for instance, seeing a woman stop her farming work, her digging, go under a tree and give birth to a baby, rest for a few minutes, put the baby on her back with a shawl wrapped round it, and carry on working. To them it was just part of nature.

The missionaries also brought division by introducing a divide between Catholics and Protestants. Every football match was between Protestants and Catholics. If a chief of an area – I remember one very nice man called William Biteyi – was a Catholic, the Protestants wouldn't speak to him because of this. It was all very strange.

I moved on and was invited by a farmer to visit his farm on a hill. He and some elders and I sat in a circle and they passed round a pipe of peace. We all took a puff of the pipe – I don't know what was in it – and then they offered some banana beer in a gourd. There was such a wonderful atmosphere of unity, which I've rarely experienced: just everybody at one. When it was time for me to go they gave me more gifts, and I had to walk back these 7 miles or so to the little truck that had brought me. And as I walked I suddenly heard from behind a great chorus of women's voices, and the women rushed either side of me, past me, and stopped. Then I walked on and through them. These waves continued all the way back to the road.

When I got back home I completed my treatment for this documentary. Then I was asked by a Colonel Dugdale to take a crew out to cover Britain's first detonation of an atom bomb on the South Sea island of Monte Bello. If I'd gone I wouldn't have been able to continue with the Uganda project, so I didn't. Whereupon Crown Film Unit was closed down by the government, and the Uganda documentary came to nothing.

Out of the blue I got a phone call from Grierson. 'Cyril, what's happening to your African film?' I told him that Crown had closed down and that it had been cancelled. 'Well, come and make it for Group 3.' And he arranged, that very day, for me to meet Monty Slater, the writer. I knew him from his book *Once a Jolly Swagman*, which I think was made into a film, and for doing the libretto for *Peter Grimes*, Benjamin Britten's opera, which I admired very much. He lived right where I'd been at school in Highgate, on the corner there. And this is how built up the screenplay for *Man of Africa*: I used to go and see him of a morning and we talked, then in the afternoon he wrote on his own, posting that day's work to me so I received it the following morning. Then I rang him and gave him my comments on what he'd written, and we'd arrange to meet the next morning to talk about the next bit.

The Union required a crew to be a minimum of twelve people. I was able to persuade them, through my contacts with Craig and also the head of the directors branch, Bob Atwoll, to agree to a unit of six. And so Denny Densham, Ronnie Spencer, Arthur Wooster, a two-man sound crew and I went out to live in the bush. The response of the pygmies was so enchanting. We were working with people who were not actors, people who didn't know what cinema was, and I was getting performances. My Oxford experience of dance, ballet and mime certainly helped.

I had a great partnership with cameraman Denny Densham. I want to say how important it is, the relationship that a director has with his cameraman, and I've been very lucky with Denny – unfortunately no longer with us – and the other great cameramen I've worked with – Freddy Young and Freddie Francis, among others. I had some great partnerships.

The music in the film, apart from the indigenous pygmy and other local music, was composed by Malcolm Arnold, later Sir Malcolm.

My general assistant and interpreter was a young man called Seperia Umpambara – known as Sep – whose father had been a chief; he was like a civil servant. Every day brought a new challenge. I remember I was very worried when we came in the story to the death of an old man; I was concerned that he wouldn't agree to play dead. But he said, 'I'm a very lucky man – I shall know how many people come to my funeral.'

Throughout we had Grierson's unqualified support. He would send us notes, by telegram, about the rushes: 'all feel very privileged to see first rushes . . .', 'camera action performance excellent . . .', 'like reserved degree of nakedness . . .', 'watch carefully for dead wood – I make this point only because of the excellence of the majority of your shooting . . .'. I was very lucky to have been taken under his wing.

'*Katcha Kurabango*' was the nickname the pygmies gave me: it means 'the one with the long neck'. Well, I don't know that I have a particularly long neck, but it was certainly on the line when I got home. Wielding the axe was Michael Balcon. He was making a series of movies with Harry Watt in Kenya; these were not about Africans, but featured British actors with Africans in the background. In contrast Grierson had produced a film with an all-black cast of local people and no actors – and what with the pygmies and the music and one thing and another, Michael just felt it wasn't moviemaking: he thought nobody would want to see it. You also have to remember that in those early years after the war the black population of this country was pretty insignificant – so he thought there would be no natural audience for the film. And this was our distributor: Grierson's Group 3 was part of the Film Finance Corporation, whose films were distributed by Michael. I was crushed, as I felt the film had a powerful emotional message. It had cost £38,000 to make, and I completely disagreed that it would not recover its money.

Grierson took *Man of Africa* to the Berlin Film Festival and the Cannes Film Festival, and in both cases it was well reviewed. *Man of Africa* was the last film delivered before Group 3 went into liquidation. The film was cut down to a kind of documentary length, a travelogue, a support programme, and Grierson, Montague Slater and I had our names removed from the credits.

I think it was Brian Taylor who many years later discovered that a complete copy of *Man of Africa* was held at the British Film Institute. Through that and the help of Sir John Terry, who had been on the board of Group 3, we were able to get another copy, and between the two of them we reconstructed the version that has since played in several film festivals to much acclaim. The film was acquired for a period by Channel 4 but they never showed it.

Grierson was quoted as saying, 'If I am to be remembered, I would like it to be for *Man of Africa*.' I share that sentiment, and it remains my mission to have the film shown in memory of John Grierson. It still remains the only film made entirely with black non-actors. The only one. It was interesting to read recently about black film producers trying to make films with black actors and still not being able to get the finance. We read today about how Hollywood dominates the business and British films can't get shown – and that's what was happening then.

Sep, my assistant on *Man of Africa*, went on to become the Minister for Trade. He came to England and involved me and my family in sourcing clothes and alcohol, in competition with the people who had been providing these things for the Ugandan government before. But when we provided him with all this information he rejected it. When I asked him why, he said, 'Well, look how much work we did for you for *Man of Africa* and it was never shown.' Then there was this big revolution in Uganda. Amin came in and tried to shoot the government of the time. Sep feigned death, and managed to escape to Kenya. Despite the political ups and downs we remained warm friends.

When one of the girls who took part in the film came over to England to study to be a teacher, she rang me and asked if she could see me. When we met she told me that the night before she left Uganda she'd gone to a party, met somebody she didn't know and had become pregnant. So now she was landed with this teacher training course and was expecting a baby – what could she do? I arranged for her to get an extension on her stay through the Colonial Office, and arranged with the Unmarried Mothers Association for her to be looked after in hospital and so forth. Denny Densham and I became godparents when the baby boy was born. And it was wonderful: the Unmarried Mothers Association really looked after everything, caring for the baby while she completed her studies. Eventually she returned to Uganda, her child with her.

With the demise of Group 3 there was nothing for me to go on to. When the disaster happened – when *Man of Africa* was cut down to this ten- or fifteen-minute documentary – Grierson said to me, 'Cyril, you should do what no other director has done. Choose your favourite film and go and visit the director and work alongside him for a film.' I thought about this for a while. One film I was deeply impressed with was called *Le Diable au Corps*, which I'd seen at one of the cinemas which were totally committed to showing foreign films with subtitles. *Le Diable au Corps* was directed by Claude Autant-Lara. It had Gerard Philipe as a young undergraduate, who falls in love with a married woman, played by Micheline Presle, during the war while her husband is away. I found the way the film was made, especially its flowing camerawork, was very much my style. So I went over to Paris and looked up Claude Autant-Lara, who was living in a very bourgeois flat. He told me that he no longer made films that way, but used a lot of back-projection instead. That evening I went to see one of his new films, and I found it appalling. There was no feeling of movement; it was all – as he said – back-projection. And so I didn't go further with Claude Autant-Lara. Funnily enough, many years later I was working on a television series with an actress, Yvonne Coulette, who was married to a French cameraman. He came onto the set one day and I was introduced to him – and he turned out to be the cameraman and camera operator of *Le Diable au Corps*. When I said to him that I thought the camerawork had a wonderful flow, he told me that the director didn't have anything to do with the camerawork.

Despite the heartache associated with it, *Man of Africa* confirmed to me that I had a gift. I was determined to find another film to direct.

Devil on Horseback, 1953

Finally a project came up. Grierson and I made a film based on the life of Lester Piggott, called *Devil on Horseback*; I collaborated with an author, Neil Patterson, on the final script. I went up to Perth in Scotland where he lived, and it was a great experience working with him. Again Grierson was very enthusiastic about the film, but a conflict with Michael Balcon arose once more. Balcon was making another film about a jockey, a boy jockey, called *The Rainbow Jacket*.

Michael's notes on our film were extensive but Sid Stone, our very astute and experienced editor, told me to take no notice and leave it to him. He made one cut, of Googie Withers and John McCullum entering a house, just a matter of seconds. When we showed the film to Michael for a second time he said, 'Oh, it's so improved now, it's marvellous, very good.'

Well, the two jockey films came out at the same time and all the reviews favoured ours. Richard Kish, of the Australian Consolidated Press wrote to me:

> Dear Cyril Frankel,
> I also cannot resist telling you how infinitely better *Devil on Horseback* is than *The Rainbow Jacket*. If you want a classic example of how to mishandle human relationships, take a gander at the Ealing film, however it will make money, though it's a shame that even Ealing could think of turning out a job like it.

This is from a director friend:

My Dear Cyril,
Just a line to congratulate you on *Devil on Horseback*, every minute of which I enjoyed enormously. I think it's a remarkable achievement on the part of everyone concerned, particularly so because to the best of my knowledge neither Grierson, Denny or yourself are keen on horses! I saw it a few days after *Conquest of Wings* and can't tell you what a relief it was to see real people with real emotions and a good script.

Michael Balcon had been very kind to me when I first started out, and I can't say very much against him, but I became caught up in his conflict with Grierson and Group 3. I remember a telling anecdote from his daughter Jill, who married the poet C. Day Lewis. She said in a radio interview that when her father retired he had this farm at the top of a hill, and how thrilled he was to be able to stand there and look 360 degrees around and see that everything belonged to him. Unfortunately people who had been very loyal to him, some for over forty or more years, like Harold Mason at Ealing, had nothing when their contracts finished. Such is life . . .

Make Me an Offer, 1954 (comedy with Peter Finch)

I made one final film with Group 3 before it was closed, and it's one of my favourites. I so enjoyed working with Peter Finch. When we started I met his wife Tamara, a Russian girl who had been in the Bolshoi or Kirov Ballet; she was lovely. Peter said, 'I've told her, for the next six weeks I'm married to you.'

I used to collect him in the morning from Dolphin Square, where he and his family lived, and drive him to Beaconsfield, and that was fine. He had this incredible ability to not even read a page of the script but take it in just by looking at it. And he knew it. He never had to sit down and repeat and learn the script. Peter was Australian. He'd come over to this country because he was more or less adopted by Laurence Olivier and Vivian Leigh when they went to Australia. He had a reputation as a drinker – but he would never drink during working hours. Coming back from Beaconsfield was something else, of course! As we came along Western Avenue Peter would say, 'Oh Cyril, at the next corner, if you don't mind, I'd just like to have . . . one.' So we'd stop and we'd have 'one' – and he'd probably want to have three. Then we'd move on, and after another few roundabouts he'd say, 'Oh, that's a lovely place, let's stop there!' It took so long to get him home . . . Apart from the fact that I was driving, I wasn't a drinker in that sense, but even so Peter made me promise that when the film was finished I'd go out with him on a 'binge'. The day after we wrapped we went out for lunch. At 3pm the pubs had already closed so I thought, well I'm safe, but Peter said, 'I know a little club in Soho.' On we went, drinking right the way through to the evening, and he was literally, I mean literally, under the table. Amazingly I was still sober. I managed to get him back to Dolphin Square and Tamara said, 'I wasn't worried because I knew he was with you.'

Drink was more of a problem for another member of the cast, Wilfred Lawson, a wonderful actor and a lovely man who had played Eliza Doolittle's father in *Pygmalion*. In the afternoon, after lunch in a bar, he couldn't remember his words – so I always worked with him in the mornings. Lawson went on to do a play at the Savoy Theatre with Trevor Howard, called *The Devil's General*. They both drank. The play was supposed to finish by eleven o'clock – I think it started at 7.30 or 8p.m. – but on one occasion by twenty past twelve all the stagehands had gone and they were drivelling on, inventing dialogue; it was incredible . . . A few of the audience were still there.

The child actor I worked with on *Make Me an Offer* was Richard O'Sullivan, who became very well known on television in the 1970s; I worked with him subsequently on other films. And the other person who was charming was Ernest Thesinger: a great character, and a wonderful man to work with.

Peter Finch had heard a rumour that Thesinger always wore a string of pearls under his clothes. Of course Peter was determined to see them, and eventually persuaded Thesinger to show him. I remember a story Thesinger told. 'I was on a train, and I was sitting in my seat in the corner by the window. It was quite crowded, but on came a man who was rather effeminate who kind of chatted to everybody, and looked at me a lot. Anyhow, when he got out the other two people in the carriage said to me, "You know what he was, don't ya?" And I said, "Well, no . . . I don't know. What was he?" And they replied, "He was stagestruck."' And so the word 'stagestruck' became synonymous for homosexual.

Peter's wife in *Make Me an Offer* was played by the lovely actress Rosalie Crutchley. I had admired her very much when I was at Oxford and she was playing with Deborah Kerr and Pamela Brown at the Playhouse. I liked her so much: she had a warmth that went with the part, much to the disappointment of the so-called producer of the film, Bill Lipscomb. He wanted someone who was totally unsuited to the part, because she was famous for having an affair with a well-known actor called Godfrey Tearle. Tearle had passed on and left the actress some money, and Lipscomb, rather of the age of Tearle, said he thought this lady would add something. But as John Baxter, who was line producer (as it is called these days) of Group 3 said, 'Oh, he's just got hot pants.'

A fellow director, Wolf Rilla, head of ACT (the Film Makers' Union) at one time, wrote to me:

> Dear Cyril Frankel,
> I feel I must write to congratulate you on *Make Me an Offer*, which I found a most moving and beautifully made film. I am of course as jealous as hell because it is a much better picture than my own, *Blue Peter*, the release of which I have yet to suffer. Nevertheless I am henceforth your fan. I thought *Make Me an Offer* was one of the best cast and acted films that I have seen for years and your own mark on it distinctive, imaginative, and full of that quality that gets the best out of admittedly a good cast and a good script. I do hope that it will carry its own rewards for you and tycoons will queue up to make you offers, all over the place.
> Yours sincerely, Wolf Rilla

But they didn't. Group 3 closed and I was out of work.

Chapter 7

The Film Years 1954–1966

first met Lucie Rie, the Austrian potter, in 1954. Having made *Man of Africa* I was looking for some decent African art, but all I could find was market stuff. I had a couple of African instruments, a drum and a very nice thing that the Africans threw up and down, containing corn or maize – but I wanted something special. I happened to be cutting through Mayfair, from Wardour Street to Edgware Road, and went up Davies Street, where there was a gallery called the Berkeley. In the window there were wonderful African masks. I imagined I couldn't afford them, but I thought I'd see how much they were. As I got to the glass door I saw a poster: 'Pots by Lucie Rie'. I knew the name Lucie Rie because when Brian and I had shared a flat in Maida Vale for a few months we'd been to Heals to buy Danish furniture: during the war Britain hadn't made furniture, so it was all continental stuff. On that visit I'd seen coffee cups and salad bowls that I admired with a little label 'Lucie Rie'. So I thought I'd have a look – and was completely captured by a little conical rice bowl. When I asked how much it was I was told 6 guineas. On my Crown Film Unit wage this was well out of my league. So I started back to the door . . . then turned around, and there was the pot, and it said, 'Buy me.' So I bought it.

I took it home and put in on the shelf – I was then living in Eccleston Square with John and Susan Allison. John's friend, the Canadian painter Stephen Andrews, had an English friend who was a painter in New York, Stella Snead. Stella came to

London, came up to visit and said, 'Oh, you've got a pot by Lucie Rie. I'm having dinner with her tomorrow; she's a close friend of mine.' I said I'd love to meet her. There were two other people there as well, Jean Ciancimino and Hortensia Ciancimino, daughter of a Musical Hall impressionist called Afrique, who sold antiques, and they said they'd like to go as well. So we were invited for coffee the following week. I stood back and let them do all the talking, just admiring the beauty of this woman. When the party broke up I asked if I could come and see her again.

Over a period of time I managed to acquire several works of Lucie's. I was, to begin with, 'a client', later 'a collector', then gradually 'a friend'; eventually, in her words, I became 'a piece of the furniture', and I got to know her very well.

Between 1954 and 1955 I spent a lot of time painting walls in Brian's flat in Maida Vale – until I was introduced to Robert Clark.

It's Great To Be Young, 1955
Robert Clark, in my opinion, was the biggest contributor to British film in this period – a bigger influence than J. Arthur Rank – and has not been given the credit he deserves. He was a producer at Associated British and a friend of David De Yong, my brother Leslie's father-in-law. Robert had just made *Dambusters* when he came to the opening of *Make Me an Offer* in Leicester Square; and he gave me five scripts to read. They were so awful that I threw them in the corner. It was only later, when I thought I'd better send them back, that I realised there was one I hadn't looked at – a musical. It was called *Youth Orchestra Story* and when I read it I realised I wanted to make it. So I met Victor Skutetsky, the producer, who had been a filmmaker in Berlin: he was an absolutely delightful man.

The film was renamed *It's Great to Be Young*, and it was great fun to make. I thought the best person for the lead role was Trevor Howard. When I went to his home on a Sunday I found both him and his wife drunk, so we asked Kenneth Moore instead. Ken wasn't available, but he met John Mills at his golf club and encouraged him to take the part. John Mills's wife thought he should stick to officer-type roles – to be more certain of his knighthood – but Ken's praise of the script helped, and Johnny was persuaded.

Richard O'Sullivan worked with me again. I found working with children exhilarating. My experience in Africa, working with non-actors, and my earlier days of appreciation of the interpretation of music were great resources, as they proved to be on other films to follow.

The greatest pleasure was working with Victor, who was a true professional. We very often used to travel back to London together – he lived near Paddington – and end up in a pub on Star Street. As I've already said I didn't want to drink at that time, as I just wanted to get home; but Victor always ordered half a bottle of champagne . . . and that was the end of the working day. It was a colourful pub. There was a lady who had come up from the country who would get you anything you wanted. And I'm not just talking of butter and eggs – although she always had a lovely wicker basket full of cream and butter and eggs. If you wanted a threesome or an any-kind-of-some she could arrange it.

It's Great to Be Young was a success all over the world, and I got more fan letters about it than any other film I had made. Robert Clark was delighted. I was invited to dinner with him and his family in Hendon and was offered a full contract with Associated British. A film I particularly wanted to make was based on a novel called *Behold Thy Daughter* by Neil Paterson, who wrote the final screenplay for *Devil on Horseback*. Robert agreed that this would be the next film we would produce.

And then, as I'd seen on other occasions, everything changed. Robert made a speech at the British Film Producers Association in Piccadilly, saying that the Americans were dominating the business too much. This was reported to Jack Warner, and within twenty-four hours Robert Clark was out. Jimmy Wallace, the administrative director of Associated British, called me in and said, 'Cyril, I'm afraid whatever arrangements you made with Robert Clark no longer apply.' It was a terrible shock to Robert, and he didn't live long afterwards. As far as I'm concerned Associated British Picture Corporation *was* Robert Clark.

No Time for Tears, 1956/7

Despite this setback Jimmy Wallace offered me *No Time for Tears* for Associated British. The script was set in a children's hospital. The writer, Anne Burnaby, was the daughter of a well-known character actor. Although I didn't work with her on the script, she was extremely happy with the interpretation I brought to it. Anna Neagle played the matron, in her first film in over twenty years not directed by her husband, Herbert Wilcox. She lived above my parents in Park Lane. I enjoyed working with her: she was a highly intelligent lady and used her intellect to define her performance. She was thrilled to be playing opposite Antony Quayle, who was a very distinguished Shakespearian and West End actor. Her husband, Herbert Wilcox, advised me to get her tired so she'd do something unexpected. She has a very dramatic scene with Angela Baddeley, which I was really impressed with. It was at least a three minute take, which I filmed many times. I rejoiced in the rushes the next day: Anna's performance was riveting.

We also cast Dame Flora Robson and Joan Sims, who was a great character. She lived round the corner from me, and we used to have lots of laughs. And again I found myself working with children. The twins in the film were the sons of one of the Boulting Brothers twins.

Alive and Kicking, 1958

In my next film I had a trio of wonderful ladies – Dame Sybil Thorndike, Kathleen Harris and Estelle Winwood. Estelle lived in New York – although she was English and married to an Englishman. She shared a home with Tallulah Bankhead. When I went to New York in the early '60s I was entertained by both of them. Tallulah had everything beige: the walls were beige; she wore beige; she had a black butler in a beige uniform. But she was delightful and, oh, she was so funny. She was reading a script, then threw it in the corner and said, 'Rubbish! My fans would never agree for me to play this part.' I saw the title of it: *Sweet Bird of Youth.*

Sybil Thorndike was one of the few actresses whom I visited backstage, having been so impressed by her performance in a play called *Family Reunion.* She and Kathleen Harris made a lovely team. Kathleen was well known for her warmth and humour.

We cast Stanley Holloway too – a marvellous man. He had played for me in *On the Fiddle,* and I so admired him in the stage version of *My Fair Lady.*

It was on *Alive and Kicking* that I found Richard Harris. The celebrated theatre director Michael Macowan, who's no longer alive, was in charge of the London Academy of Dramatic Art, where I had been casting. I told him, 'I've found a wonderful actor – one of your students.' He asked who and I told him

Richard Harris. And his face fell . . . no doubt because Richard was difficult with certain authorities, but he certainly wasn't with me. I found him a wonderful warm and affectionate person, and a delight to work with. We remained friends. I planned to make another film with him in Australia, produced by Michael Deeley, but the Australian company that was interested withdrew. But there we are – that's the thing with the film business, isn't it?

It was through Michael Macowan that I met Iris Warren, a great influence on me. She had been, or was, the voice teacher at all three Stratfords – Stratford-upon-Avon, Stratford, Connecticut and Stratford, Ontario. She had a marvellous technique of getting the voice centred, and taught many famous actors in this country. I asked her to train me so that I could use the technique with other people as a director, not as an actor, and went to weekly lessons with her at Wigmore Hall. She got you in the right posture, made you conscious of your breathing and then added a sound to the breathing. So when I was working with an amateur I could get them to speak truthfully. One of the great things she taught me was that if you have a line, any line, let's say 'to be or not to be', and you just say 'to be or not to be', it isn't coming from *there* – but if you whisper it on the breath only, and then speak it, it's different. You cut out the intellect. I've been able to use that throughout my career, particularly when working with non-actors and children.

I introduced Iris to Maharishi, and she then introduced many of her pupils to him, including Vidal Sassoon and Russ Conway. When she sadly died of cancer, Vidal accompanied me to her funeral in Camden Town.

She Didn't Say No, 1958
On my next film I worked with another fine actress, Eileen Herlie. She had played Gertrude to Olivier's *Hamlet* in his film and *The Eagle has Two Heads* in the West End. She was one of our top actresses and absolutely lovely – but after she made this film she married an American, went to America, and has never been heard of since.

She Didn't Say No was originally called *We Are Seven*, but the Americans who had been supervising everything at Associated British since Robert Clark was thrown out said that wasn't not commercial. It's a story of a woman who has five children, all by different fathers, and what they all get up to. At the end of the film she marries one of the fathers. It was meant to be set in

Ireland – so we found our locations near Galway and started to organise things. But the Bishop of Galway insisted on reading the script, and when he found out it was about illegitimate children he told us we'd no cooperation from anybody in Galway. Remembering my childhood trips to Cornwall, I thought the countryside there would do equally well, so I switched the locations to outside Falmouth. When I arrived one of the first things I did was go to the house where my old nanny, Henrietta Lelean, was living. When I got there and met the owner of the house – Henrietta had the ground floor – she told me that she was in hospital somewhere. So I had to find out which hospital she was in. Luckily Eleanor, the girl I used to go to barn dances with, who had introduced me to Sadler's Wells Ballet, was a telephonist at the telephone exchange, and through her I found out that Nurse was in Redruth Hospital. So at the end of shooting days I took a car and visited her. When I was back in London I sent her honeysuckle *eau de cologne* from Floris in Jermyn Street, because that was her favourite perfume. I had to keep on going backwards and forwards between the studio and locations, so I was able to visit her to within days of her passing. That was important somehow – for her and for me.

The film was a great hit at the Brussels Festival, despite a poor reception for other films:

> . . . the festival opened with a gala performance of a Carol Reed picture, but far from achieving the success it had in London *The Key* met with a strange lack of understanding on the part of the critics. There was a much better reception for *Dunkirk* and for Cyril Frankel's Irish comedy *She Didn't Say No*, an endearing little film in which Miss Eileen Herlie is seen as the mother of six illegitimate children.

I cast an unknown Sean Connery in this film, having seen a play on television called *Requiem for a Heavyweight*, and thinking that this young actor was rather special. Within about three weeks of starting to shoot his agent rang and asked if I would release him as he'd had an offer from 20th-Century Fox to make films in Hollywood. Reluctant as I was, I couldn't stop him from going. So off he went to Hollywood to make a film with Lana Turner, which fizzled, and another, which was never shown, and came back. I was to get another chance to work with him later.

School for Scoundrels, 1959/1960

As a contract director at Associated British I was assigned this novel by Stephen Potter (which I liked very much), by the production administrator, Jimmy Wallace. I met the producer, Hal Chester, whom I recognised as one of the Dead End Kids, and he left me to cast the film with casting director Robert Leonard. We assembled a fine cast: Alastair Sim, Terry-Thomas, Ian Carmichael (with whom I had been associated when we were providing entertainments in the army), the delightful actress Janette Scott (daughter of Thora Hird), Dennis Price, Peter Jones, Edward Chapman and John Le Mesurier.

Then I went off to find the locations. One morning I had a call from Jimmy, inviting me to his office in Golden Square, Soho. Jimmy said, 'Cyril, I'm sorry to tell you that these days actors have a lot of power, and as Terry-Thomas doesn't want to work with you we've had no alternative but to engage another director. Hal has arranged for Robert Hamer to take over.' I was shocked, but I had a great respect for Hamer, who had directed *Kind Hearts and Coronets*, that fine film with Alec Guinness. Jimmy told me he'd find another script for me soon, so it wasn't the end of the world.

In a few weeks shooting started on location with Hamer. After about three or four days I was telephoned by William Whittaker, associated producer, who had worked with me on *No Time for Tears*. He'd been in the military and simply ordered me to report for duty next morning; apparently Robert Hamer had been drunk the previous evening and was still drunk. I said, 'Wait a minute, do you know the background to this?' He repeated his order. I told him I'd speak to Jimmy Wallace – which I did – and agreed to speak to Robert Hamer first. When I went to his home in Kensington he was still intoxicated and near tears. He blamed Hal for driving him to drink, and begged me to take over. As far as he was concerned Chester was impossible to work with. The phone rang. It was a friend of his, Diana Morgan, the writer, and he broke down speaking to her. I made him an offer. I would take over for one week, provided he received medical treatment and then returned. I reported our conversation to Jimmy Wallace, and told him my decision.

Next day I found the film unit in a state of total depression, and had to work hard to pull them together. We were on location at a block of flats in Hendon, and within two days were back on schedule again, which raised morale. Then we moved location and I came face to face with Terry-Thomas. I asked him, face to face, whether he was content to work with me – and he enthusiastically spoke of his long admiration of my work. It emerged that Terry-Thomas's agent also represented Robert Hamer, who at the time was unemployed, and he, together with Hal, reckoned that Hamer's name would be an asset. Regrettably, after a week Hamer was still refusing to accept medical help, and thus I continued to direct.

On one location I filmed two actors running and jumping on a bus. Together with zoom lens I 'covered' the sequence, and we were ready to wrap up and move to the next site. Then a car drew up with Hal Chester and two guests. He called out, 'I want a close-up.' I told him that we had filmed close-ups. 'I'm the producer. I want a close-up.' In an effort to impress his guests he ranted on. I walked towards him. 'See that blue MG? Unless you stop interfering I'll be off.' He continued in the same vein, so I strode to my car and drove back to the studio. I went to the studio manager's office – Vaughan Dean – and said I'd resigned. His face fell. Oh no, Cyril! I'd told him, I hadn't resigned, but I insisted that if I were to continue to direct Hal Chester would not be allowed to enter the set or approach the unit. This was agreed and I continued to complete the film. The crew and all the actors were totally supportive. When the film was shown my name was not on the credits: listed as director was Robert Hamer.

Several decades later the National Film Theatre held a festival of Robert Hamer films, including *School for Scoundrels*. Ian Carmichael introduced the film and stated emphatically that it was not directed by Robert Hamer but by Cyril Frankel. As a result it's usually published now with a credit to me. I never saw or spoke to Hal Chester again, neither have I heard a good word about him.

Never Take Sweets from a Stranger, 1960

I regard my next film as among my best work. *Never Take Sweets from a Stranger* is unfortunately never shown nowadays, despite the fact that its theme of paedophilia continues to be very relevant, and indeed the film would be relevant.

Never Take Sweets highlights the fact that a director's relationship with the cameraman – and particularly the camera operator – is frightfully important. You have to be able to speak the same language without a word. The cameramen I have worked with have been a very important part of my career. I was lucky with *Man of Africa* and several documentaries to work with Denny Densham; we went on to make *Devil on Horseback* and *Make Me an Offer* together. With *It's Great to Be Young* I had to have a contract cameraman from Associated British, but by the time of *Never Take Sweets*, a Hammer film, I was able to pick and choose, and I chose Freddie Francis. He did a wonderful job and we got on really well: it was a lasting relationship. I later worked for his wife Doreen, who had a company called Francis Montague that made commercials. Freddie had told her to use me, basically setting it up. We did quite a few – getting a Cannes prize for a cigarette advert.

Never Take Sweets and *Man of Africa* are what I regard as my 'worthy work'. But, just like *Man of Africa, Never Take Sweets* suffered in distribution. It was made in collaboration with Columbia, who regarded it as the best film Hammer had ever made for them, but when they tried to show it in the States the Catholic Women's Guild had it banned. It was one of those films that just disappeared . . . It's a bizarre business.

Grounds for Divorce: Love, 1961

For my next film I went back to Germany. The comedy *Grounds for Divorce: Love* was produced by Arthur Brauner of CCC Films. He had come from a concentration camp and somehow gathered enough money to buy the old factory where they had produced gas for the camps. And that was CCC Films.

Of course, the problem with making films in Germany, which cropped up again when I worked with Brian Taylor on *Trygon Factor*, was that the Germans had this thing about getting a star actor, or someone they think is a star actor. So you find you're landed with an actor who has contractual script rights. I had had the script for *Trygon Factor* beautifully doctored by Kingsley Amis, but Stewart Grainger wouldn't speak the lines. He rewrote it. He would rewrite it overnight. The same thing happened with O.W. Fischer on *Grounds for Divorce: Love*. He was Germany's number one actor, and had his own director with him all the time. I had to meet him at Munich's Four Seasons Hotel before going to Berlin. He admired my English suit – the material – and asked if I would like some pâté de foie gras sandwiches. I'd never had pâté de foie gras sandwiches. He lived in Switzerland with something like forty cats. Oh dear, never mind . . .

The film was well received in Germany: '. . . after running for three weeks, we can report to you the film goes very well with the public. The critiques are good and we hope this success continues . . .'

Don't Bother to Knock, 1962

In 1962 I was approached again to do a film at Associated British. *Don't Bother to Knock* starred Richard Todd and the wonderful actress Judith Anderson, known nowadays for having played Mrs Danvers in Hitchcock's *Rebecca*, but whom I had first seen playing Lady Macbeth.

Playing one of the young girls was another discovery of mine, Elke Sommer, whom I had tested for *Grounds for Divorce: Love* but not used. I remember visiting her at the Mayfair Hotel, and her changing in front of me without a second thought. Stark naked, she said to me, 'You might as well see what you've got to sell.'

The music for this comedy was composed by Elisabeth Lutyens, who'd worked with me on *Never Take Sweets* – a lovely person. She went on to become a cult figure for her horror movie work, which I remember her saying brought in more income than all her classical work put together. I can believe it.

Another friend on *Don't Bother to Knock* was editor Anne Coates. Anne has been a lifelong friend. I remember going with her to see Marlene Dietrich do her cabaret act at the Café du Paris. It was sold out, of course, but she knew we'd get in. She went up to the box office and said, 'My brother was here last night and he spent £90.' Immediately a table was put in the front for us! I thought Marlene was tremendous – a wonderful artist. Later I went with Anne to the premiere of a film she had edited for David Lean, *Ryan's Daughter*. I was a great admirer of Lean, but I thought it too long. I remember cameraman Freddie Young telling me that the film took two years to make. The weather would be perfect for shooting and he'd go to Lean's caravan and say, 'David, David, we can shoot,' and Lean would reply, 'Oh clear off, you old bugger, *I'm* not ready.'

When We Dead Awake

After *Don't Bother to Knock* I did a play in Dublin at the Gate Theatre. This is what really got me into theatre. The play was *When We Dead Awake* by Ibsen. It had a lovely cast. Anew McMaster was the most celebrated Shakespearean actor in Ireland. Barbara Chilcott was one of the Davies family from Canada and she'd been playing in the West End here. Very beautiful glamorous lady. William Marshall was a black American actor – very very good. Magdalena Nicol was Brazilian and I had seen her do a play by Lorca here in London called *Yerma* and was so impressed that I did what I rarely do, go backstage and tell her so – and we became very good friends. She played the lead, on the insistence of Maureen Halligan, who otherwise would have liked the lead herself and who financed to a great degree this production. Maureen had played for me in at least two films, and was a great admirer. She later moved to the United States. The play had marvellous notices.

While working on this play in Dublin I met Ricki Huston, who was married to John Huston. Ricki Huston was another gloriously beautiful lady, one of the most beautiful women I ever met. We used to have dinner together, go to the movies together. She encouraged me to make a film on Colette and her stories. And she introduced me to people in Ireland.

In Ireland, John Huston had this huge house full of statues and I don't know what, but the family – his wife and two children – lived in the lodge. I met Ricki through the painter Morris Graves, who's no longer alive, who also lived in Dublin and whom I wanted to meet. Maureen Halligan had introduced me to Morris Graves, who in turn said you must meet Ricki Houston.

Ricki and I really got on like a house on fire. John Huston was then away in Athens doing something, preparing something. Ricki used to write his scripts for him, not for any credit. Anyhow, later, I'm casting some film and Robert Leonard, who was the casting director at Associated British, comes in and says, 'Oh I'm so sorry, Cyril, Ricki was killed in a car accident.' I was very upset.

I later bumped into her daughter Anjelica in Los Angeles. Anjelica, who was a teenager when her mother died, has written a lot about her life and her early life, but never once mentions her mother – although she talks about her father a lot. Most bizarre.

On the Fiddle, 1963 (in America *Operation Snafu*)

After the play in Dublin, when I was living in a flat in Chelsea, I had pleurisy and was rather unwell. It was at this time that I was approached by Ben Fisz, a producer who later made *The Battle of Britain*. He offered me a comedy script, *On the Fiddle*, which reflected very many of my own Army experiences. It was by Harold Buchman, and was based on *Stop at a Winner*, a novel by R.M. Delderfield.

There was a part in it for a gypsy. I immediately said that, having heard he was back in England, I'd like Sean Connery for the role. Ben told me he was just hanging around the Pinewood canteen, and that nobody would use him because he couldn't act. I said that I knew he *could* act. 'Naah. Hollywood threw him out, you know. I'd prefer you had Bernard Bresslaw.' Now Bernard was marvellous in the right part, but I thought he would be too broad for this role. 'No, I think Sean Connery's right.' And Ben replied, 'Well, if you think you can get a performance out of him . . .' So I arranged for Sean to come and have a drink with me, and I told him about the script. When he heard the part was a gypsy, he said he couldn't do it if we were going to make fun of gypsies (which we weren't), as he was half-gypsy himself.

Anyway, Sean and Ben agreed and Sean gave a lovely performance. We shot the film at Shepperton. Halfway through Ben came onto my set with Harry Saltzman and asked me if I thought Sean could play Bond. Well, in those days nobody knew what James Bond was going to be; we guessed it was going to be another *The Saint* or one of those television personality-driven series. I said I thought he could do it standing on his head reading a newspaper. And, of course, he got the part.

It disappoints me that, although there are many books written about James Bond and Sean Connery, Sean has never shown any appreciation for *On the Fiddle*, even though at the time it took more money worldwide than *Dr No* ($26.9m to *Dr No*'s $25.6m). Certainly its success was helped by Sean being in it – it went round the world on the back of *Dr No* and James Bond – but it's part of his story. One day I'm sure Sean and I will meet again, as he spends quite a bit of time in Spain: I'll be able to remind him!

An actor called Michael Sarne, who did a lot of film and television work, wrote to me about the film:

Dear Cyril, I very much enjoyed *On the Fiddle* and I am ashamed to say that it was very much better than I had dared to expect [he had a small part in it]. The most interesting thing about it was, in my humble opinion, the offbeat philosophy of the film. It disregarded conventionality of the corny cinematic sort and supplied a morality and taste which is far more valid to art than any other British comedy I have seen. It's a terrific film. Thank you Cyril.

The Witches, 1964 (in America *The Devil's Own*)

Joan Fontaine was represented in England by Dennis Van Thal of London Management, who was also my agent. She showed him a script for a thriller that she had commissioned (it was written by Nigel Kneale and was based on a novel by Peter Curtis, *The Devil's Own*), and asked him to recommend a director. He arranged for her to meet me at a hotel off Bond Street. Of course I was thrilled to meet an Oscar-winning actress of such beauty. All I can say of our meeting is that the exchange of eyes spoke not just to me but also to her; and she instantly agreed to invite me to direct the film.

I chose an actor I admired, Alec McCowen. The script also required a leading actress opposite Joan: I had recently worked with Kay Walsh and believed she would be right. Hammer, who'd agreed to make the film, appointed a line producer who preferred Faith Brook, who'd had an affair with the late Geoffrey Tearle; the Hammer producer said he had 'a fire in his trousers' for her. But I was convinced that Kay Walsh would be the most powerful actress for the part.

All went well with the shooting. I ensured that the camera angles invariably favoured Joan, which must have disturbed Kay. On one occasion she charged up to Joan and seemed about to strike her. I stood between them and whispered to Joan to ignore it. Kay subsided and we continued to shoot. It was a wonderful experience for me to work with someone as subtle and expressive as Joan, and we remain close to this day.

At the end of shooting Joan told me she would have preferred a 'tall, dark, handsome' actor rather than Alec McCowen; but later, when he did his Biblical readings on Broadway, she was thrilled with him.

Perhaps the most successful casting was the cat. I used Barbara Woodhouse, the animal trainer who had worked with me on *Make Me an Offer*, for a pivotal scene where it was crucial the cat's hair and tail stood up as it approached the house. The cat was perfect.

The Trygon Factor, 1965

This thriller was a chance to work with my old friend from Army days, Brian Taylor. The Danziger Brothers, whom Brian had been working with, bumped into Ian Warren who had finance from Rialto Films in Denmark. The Danzigers suggested us to make the film. We collaborated with Kingsley Amis on the script, spending time with him and his wife, Elizabeth Jane Howard.

Among the leading actors were Stewart Granger, Brigitte Horney and Robert Morley. Robert insisted on having his own caravan and telephone so that he could continue his hobby of following horse racing. What I found so remarkable was that on any direction from me his facial expression would instantly change and he would express exactly what I had suggested.

The Very Edge, 1965

Elizabeth Jane Howard wrote a screenplay for me called *The Very Edge*. I knew her when I was involved in studying Ouspensky, and knew her first husband, who was a bit of a conman – as she herself says in her book *Slipstream*. In the same book she is very complimentary about me, which is rather embarrassing:

> . . . and then one of the kindest man I have known came to my rescue. Cyril Frankel was a member of the Ouspensky society. I'd first met him when he and his friend Stephen Andrews, the Canadian painter, were living with John Allison, my doctor in Eccleston Square . . . He was a film director and like so many of them was looking and waiting for something to turn up. When it did, he asked me to go and see him with a view to our working together.

The film had been set up by Anne Heywood's husband, Raymond Stross, who was only interested in making her a star. I arranged for her to study with Iris Warren. Also in the film were Jeremy Brett, a fine actor, and Richard Todd. It worked well.

Puritan to Cavalier, 1966

This is one of my best works – a TV documentary about English poetry, which ran for about forty minutes. It had fabulous reviews. The *New York Times* wrote, on 13 January 1966: 'Future monthly instalments of ESSO World Theatre will explore the cultures of many other countries. On last night's evidence the project is in excellent hands, which promises to make a prime contribution to civilised television.'

I filmed on location. We did Chaucer on Hampstead Heath, then a Shakespeare sonnet with Anna Massey and Paul Rogers; inside Kenwood House with Anna Massey and Peter Wyngarde; and finally Ralph Richardson reciting Dylan Thomas in Westminster Abbey. I loved working with Ralph: we'd first worked together in the '40s, when he recorded the commentary for *Eagles of The Fleet,* and continued our association in the '80s, with a documentary about the Old Vic. When filming was over the phone rang, and Ralph said, 'I just want to say that I thought you expressed two very rare qualities: taste and simplicity. I just want you to know that.'

I also received a lovely letter from Anna Massey after the shoot:

> Darling Cyril,
> I cannot tell you how sad I am that those three happy weeks of working with you are over. I have never enjoyed acting so much. Your help, patience and way of working were a sheer joy and thank you simply for just everything. It is very seldom that one can feel completely free and at ease with a director. There is usually between the actor and director a gap – sometimes small – of what he wants and what he gets. With you this tension never appeared and it made what is usually painful just happy. Anyway these are all words and what I really mean is bless you and please let's work together again soon.
> Always, Anna.

I always valued the relationship between myself and actors, that *inner* relationship, which I think has characterised what I have done over the years and extends into all fields of my life.

Maharishi

When I think back over my eighty years the most important lifeline – apart from the world of entertainment – is the search for a meaning of life. I didn't find an answer in established religions. Aldous Huxley's book *The Perennial Philosophy* and also a book Alvin Bailey gave me to read about the history of the mind were very influential, and set me off on a search.

I've talked about Mrs Molineux and Iris Warren. The other person whose philosophy had a big influence on my life and my career was Maharishi. I've mentioned that I met the Romanian conductor Celibidache when I came out of the Army. He was a practising Buddhist, and would say to me, 'What is the essence of time? What is the essence of silence?' He put ideas in my head. I was living with John and Susan Allison near Victoria (I was godfather to their children), and Celibidache – who'd come over to conduct the London Philharmonic Orchestra – came over of an evening and we'd talk about philosophical Buddhist language until the early hours. I explored it, but I still didn't find the answer.

Through John Allison I met the Canadian painter Stephen Andrews, and he led me to study Ouspensky, who had been a follower of Gurdjieff. I went to a meeting of Ouspensky disciples in Wimpole Street, which was conducted by Dr Francis Roles and was all about having one's eyes open, having a wide vision and remembering yourself. When he asked if there were any questions at the end, I said, 'You told us to keep our eyes open. Can we do this with our eyes closed?' He replied, 'We're trying to wake up, not go to sleep.' That put me in my place. I never trusted the teaching. I wasn't convinced, mainly because of Mrs Molineux and my own personal experience.

There were other teachings around, and one went along to a degree. But then – when I was in Germany making *Grounds for Divorce: Love* – I received a message from John Allison in London, saying that a man who I'd want to meet was there, Maharishi, and that I must come. I was about to start filming on the Monday, and this was the Friday. So I went into the production office and told them I had to go London for the weekend but would be back on the Sunday: John had told me Maharishi was giving a lecture on Saturday. They said I couldn't possibly, because of insurance and starting the film. I said I was sorry, but I had to. I eventually convinced them that I would be back in good time and we would start the film on Monday.

So I flew to London and went to the meeting, where this shining man spoke. I was so convinced that I wanted to have his teaching that I went backstage to see him at the end. When I told him I was going back to Germany the next day there was a long silence and he asked if I was tired. I was, because I'd travelled by air that morning, but I said no. There was another long silence. Then he said, 'They will tell you what to bring. You come to where I am staying at half past eleven tonight.' When I came out there were John and Susan. 'What did he say? What did he say?' 'He said you'd know what I have to bring. I have to go to his place off Sloane Street tonight.' They produced some flowers, some fruit, a white handkerchief . . . and off I went to meet him. There was a ceremony and I was given a mantra. It took thirty or forty minutes, and I came out onto the street absolutely agog, I couldn't possibly sleep.

When I got on the aeroplane the next morning I realised I couldn't remember what I'd been taught. So once I was back in Berlin I telephoned Maharishi, and he set me on the path again. I was so taken by the result of what he called getting to the transcendental within oneself that when I heard he was going to Paris I went to Paris. But he was delayed in Lille, teaching, and I only saw him briefly before I had to get on a plane back again.

When the film had finished, a little later on, Maharishi was back in London, staying in a house overlooking the north side of Regent's Park by the zoo entrance. I used to go and talk with him in the evenings, with a group of people. While he ate – he only ate vegetables grown above the ground – we asked questions. I said, 'We're supposed to do this meditation in the morning and in the evening, but I don't have time in the morning because I'm rushing to Elstree Studios.' He replied, 'Of the two meditations, the most important is the one before activity, not after activity. What time do you get up to go to the studio?' 'I leave home at half past seven, so I'm usually up at ten to seven, quarter to seven.' He said, 'Very well. Tomorrow you will come here at half past six.'

So I did. The front door was unlocked and I went straight upstairs to his room, tapped on the door and found him sitting on the bed in a meditative position. He said, 'Sit. Meditate.' He checked to see how I was going – and finally asked if I could return the next day. This went on for about three weeks. At the end of this he said my meditation was perfect – I didn't think so – and that I didn't need to come back again. From that day forward I never had any difficulty with my meditation.

I had been worried that the early morning ride to Shepperton was when I had to prepare – to decide what I was going to shoot. Maharishi said, 'No, you do not prepare. You meditate. And then you go on to the studio and say, do this, do this, do this, shoot.' I thought I'd take him at his word, so I got in the car to go to Shepperton and to my surprise I realised I knew the script – the film I was working on was *On the Fiddle*. I didn't have to learn it; I knew it. And when I got to the location I got out of the car and asked the cameraman, his assistant and the sound man to follow me. We walked round the lake and I said, 'Right, we'll shoot here and we'll shoot there, and we will so this . . .' and from then on I've always done things in this more intuitive way. Of course the more I learnt to do this the more I began to trust my intuition, and not to be so intellectual about things. No longer did I write everything down and think it out beforehand. I realised that in my early days, when I'd worked things out in detail before shooting, I wasn't taking into account what the actors would bring.

I became very impressed with Maharishi as a being. He moved on to Rome, to set up his movement there, and when I visited the city I heard he was staying at the Grand Hotel Excelsior. I went there to find a great mob of Italians, obviously protecting him. I said that I wanted to see Maharishi – 'Oh, impossible'. 'Will you tell him, please, that Cyril from London is here.' 'It won't make any difference. You can't see him.' 'Please tell him Cyril from London is here.' Eventually the message got through and I was told that I could see him.

I went up to his room, a little rectangular room. He was sitting on the bed in his meditative position, and he asked how my meditation was. I said, 'Fine, but I have a question . . . Are you of the level of angels?' It was two in the afternoon now, in the summer, so there was a pretty bright shaft of light, and he asked me to close the shutters. So I got up and closed the shutters, and as I did so I sensed something within . . . I turned round and he was sitting there, with an enormous golden disc around him, enormous. I sank down on the floor and said, 'What is this light?'

And he said, 'You can see it, can you?' Then he went into a discourse, about how when the body is purified a charge goes through each hair.' This was the time that people were beginning to say he was taking money from the Beatles, and one thing and another – which was not true. I was totally convinced, and remain so to this day. I practise meditation regularly, and feel it's established in my being now.

These are all Maharishi notes . . . 'Personal love is concentrated universal love. Love is always selective. In the state of universal love heart flows in abundance, remains steady in fulfilment.' 'To realise God, faith does not help. Faith remains a barrier. Here innocence works. Faith put out by those who want God realisation means they remain in the *idea* of God. Faith is a sweet thing but only stands as a mountain between man and God.'

Linked to all of this was that I developed a gift of healing; although this was not directly from Maharishi. When I told him I was practising healing he said it had to be of the mind and not physical, but I'd had quite a bit of success with the physical. It came about this way. When I developed pains running down my arms and frozen fingertips I went to my doctor, my close friend John Allison. He said I had arthritis of the neck and had to wear a collar.

Well, my vanity was such that I couldn't see myself wandering around a film set with a collar. I remembered a property man called Tester, who had a home down in Haywards Heath with his family and an office in Gloucester Place, where he saw people once a week for healing. A cousin of mine, Dennis Frankel, a lawyer, who sadly died young, had introduced me to him. So I telephoned him and asked if he was still seeing people for healing. He said he was, so I went to see him. He played some relaxing music by George Shearing in the background and gave me gentle massage and so forth. When I went out I felt just the same as when I went in, but I woke up two days later totally free of pain. I really couldn't believe it. Totally free.

John rang and said, 'Cyril, you haven't come to be measured up for your neck collar.' And I told him I'd been to a healer and was better. 'Huh!' he said, 'You'll be back!' But I never went back. What I did was phone Tester again – and invited him to lunch at the restaurant I owned at this time. And I said to him, 'This seems to speak to me . . . You know, I practise meditation and one thing and another, and I'd like to develop healing if possible. What shall I do?' There was a healer called Harry Edwards who had given demonstrations at the Albert Hall – lame people leaving without their crutches, that sort of thing – and Tester recommended me to write off for his study papers. I did, and they didn't tell me anything I didn't already know. When I asked again what to do, he said, 'Don't worry, someone will turn up.' And he was right. When my bookkeeper – a very nice lady – said to me she had pain in her back, I said, 'Sit down . . .' and I'm pleased to say she got better.

At the same time the deputy Prime Minister of Cyprus, Yannis Matsis, was visiting London, and he told me he had a friend who for twenty years had been suffering with shoulder pain and had been to doctors all round the world without success. So I said I'd have a go. I did – and the following day he felt better. He introduced me to a colleague of his, 'We send you our love and warmest thanks for your kind help. I feel quite well now and I know I owe this to you. Our address is . . . Athens. Needless to say you are always welcome. With love and gratitude, George Effis B. Spirou.'

Then I treated Ken Grant, stage manager for me on several productions in Vienna. He wrote: 'Thank you also for healing my neck, for heal it did, the next day.'

Richard Grenville, an agent at London Management, came to see me and it took him nearly twenty minutes to come up the stairs. But within three weeks he was walking properly again.

Doreen Mishcon, wife of Victor, Baron Mishcon, lawyer to Diana Princess of Wales, was suffering from severe cancer:

> Dear Mr Frankel,
> After my second visit to you and the wonderful little talk about letting my spirit go free. I really feel much better – quite miraculously so – I am extraordinarily grateful to you for giving me so much of your time and also your wonderful gift of healing. Words cannot explain adequately how good it is to feel well again, to feel life flow, old vigour returning and the awful tired weakness disappearing. It's too marvellous to explain. Thank you, thank you, thank you, thank you too for taking away my fear of dying; something I think that worried me more than I realised. The relief from that fear is also a great thing . . .

What I'm really saying is that this stream of . . . the inner thing . . . is in all aspects of my life and work. Through it Steve Nelson arrived in my life. I met him through Irving Davis, a choreographer I had worked with over the years who also practised meditation. Steve decided that Irving and I had this way of life that he wanted, so, on his own, he went off and met a teacher of meditation and started to meditate. It is one of the bonds we share.

Maharishi gave me a complete way of living, a complete way of being, of realising that it is not the thinking process that is important but the distinction between intellect and transcendence. If you live according to the laws of nature, and if you meditate, it takes you to a place of silence within yourself, where you are in accord with the laws of nature. Whatever comes up from that is intuition, which you can trust.

Tester had been on the board of *Psychic News*, and later, when the man who founded and ran it died, they asked me to take over from him and become chairman. But I found the people involved were interested more in property and profit, and I wasn't really terribly enthralled by this. I just wanted to further Maharishi's teaching; by this time I was a trustee of his charity.

Chapter 8

The Television Years 1967–1977

n the latter half of the '60s there was a slump in filmmaking. But I'd caught the attention of Lew Grade. On 21 September 1966 I received this note from my agent, Dennis Van Thal: 'My dear Cyril, You'll be glad to know I continue to receive excellent comments about you and indeed yesterday when I saw Lew Grade in person he endorsed these encouraging comments. If I feel heartened by these as I do I'm sure you must be.'

I went on to make over a hundred television show episodes for Lew Grade – shows such as *Gideon's Way*, *The Baron*, *The Champions*, *Randall and Hopkirk*, *Department S*, *Jason King*, *UFO*, *The Protectors*, *The Adventurer*, *The Avengers* . . . Lew Grade said to me, 'Every time your name comes up on the screen I know I can sell it.' I was the only television director for these shows ever to be given a percentage – 2 per cent of the profits of four series: *Department S, Randall and Hopkirk, Jason King* and *The Adventurer*. Invariably I did the first one, to set the style. But of course none of these – all of which were sold around the world and have been shown on television ever since – has ever made a profit! For thirty years I received nothing, although in 2005 I received a cheque for *The Adventurer*, thirty years after it was first broadcast!

Adapting from film to television was all about speed. You're making an hour's film in nine days: in general it's 'Action! Cut! Print!'. But you still had to have a relationship with the actors –

Gene Barry, Peter Wyngarde, Kenneth Cope – I developed good relationships with many of them. And there was Dennis Spooner, who was in charge of all the scripts on *The Champions*. I liked him enormously and thought he did an excellent job.

The key thing to making a film is the unit. Camera, sound, all the props, all the property men, all the carpenters, everything, all work as a unit. And the director is the person who, as it were, creates the atmosphere for that unit to work together. A film unit isn't just a director – it is the whole crew working together.

I've been very fortunate with my crews. Perhaps when I made *It's Great to Be Young* my camera crew was not exactly hostile but slightly withdrawn: they were obviously waiting to see what I was up to. Gilbert Taylor, the cameraman, who was under contract there and for whom – initially – it was just another film, gradually came round. He went on to become the cameraman for *Alive and Kicking* and also *The Adventurer* series: he had a marvellous concept of indirect reflected light. We worked very well together. His son is a camera operator whom I worked with later and liked very much.

As I said before one of my best relationships with cameramen was with Denny Densham. Denny and I went over to America to work with ABC Television on a script that we'd developed ourselves and Lew Grade liked; we even found locations in Cyprus. But we got a cold reception, and they didn't want to go ahead with it. Instead they made it themselves, calling it *The Million Dollar Man*. Lew Grade said he couldn't do anything about it. This kind of thing is a trick of the trade, and everybody has their stories – but it was a disappointment.

On many of these programmes I was fortunate to be working alongside Ken Baker. He had been an assistant on some of my earlier films and was constant in his loyalty and enthusiasm as my first assistant director. My favourite series remains to this day *The Champions* – the concept, the beauty of our star Alexandra Bastedo . . .

Eventually the shows started to become repetitive, and the quality of writing dropped. So in the early '70s – I think 1972 – I decided to open a restaurant. My friend Phivos Yiannouka, another Cypriot friend, Andy Eftichiou, and I all contributed a bit of money, found some premises and opened it. It was off Bond Street, 10 Lancashire Court, and we called it Number 10. It was an international restaurant, with some Cypriot dishes because Phivos's sister, Jiansulla, was a wonderful cook. Kem Bennet was also a chef for us: he had had a very good restaurant in Chelsea, a famous one, and he was doing international dishes.

The restaurant was well received. In no time at all it got an Egon Ronay star. The food critics Fanny Cradock and her husband gave it a 'rave' in the *Daily Telegraph*, while Humphrey Lyttelton praised it, and the first London edition of the Michelin *Guide* included Number 10 in its recommendations. Many celebrities came, including Lili Palmer and her husband, Alec Guinness, Ava Gardner, who asked us to send her desserts by taxi, Lord Snowdon, who often came for lunch and arrived one evening, when the restaurant was quiet, with Princess Margaret – who ordered scrambled eggs! When Marlene Dietrich joined some friends at Number 10 I asked her whether she'd like a drink. 'Oil 'av a bierre' was her answer.

We had a staff of about twelve. I gradually realised that running a restaurant was very different from directing a film. The staff helped themselves. We had to count everything every day – the bottles, foods such as fillet steaks – but on the other hand we had no choice but to trust everyone, particularly when I left to do *The Adventurer* – to pay the bills at the restaurant. But there we are . . .

After two years my bank manager persuaded me that we'd lost enough and it was time to close. Nowadays Lancashire Court is blazing with light and full of restaurants – Roger Moore's son has opened one down there, which is thriving – but in the '70s a passage off Bond Street didn't attract very much evening trade, and women didn't like walking down there.

So there I was – in debt to the bank, for quite a large sum of money, and living in a house on the Grosvenor Estate with a very short lease that was coming up for renewal at a very high sum I couldn't afford. So I sold the short lease and made a little to get by, but nothing to pay off the bank. I was offered accommodation in Mayfair by a friend who worked in the Italian Embassy. Unfortunately he had a cat who resented any intrusion, and after two aggressive nights my Italian friend said, 'Cyril, I'm sorry, you must leave. My first responsibility is to the cat.'

For a couple of nights I stayed with a former waiter from Number 10, who had become a good friend of my sister Violet, who worked at the cash desk in the restaurant. Then another friend of Violet's, a truly extraordinary, kind man named Michael Obolensky, offered me a flat near Warren Street over an office that he was planning to close in about six months, as his business partner had died. I was able to move in, together with some furniture I'd had in storage. Then a few weeks later he told me that an employee of his knew of a flat in a mews near Marylebone High Street that had become vacant. I discovered who the landlords were and received the offer of a twenty-odd-year lease for something like £20,000. Because of the restaurant debt I couldn't raise the money.

At this time I was regularly visiting my friend Lucie Rie, the potter. She had a strong intuition, realised I was under some stress and wanted to know what was wrong. I admitted I needed to raise funds to buy this lease. Lucie instructed me to sell the pots of hers that I had – but I said I couldn't: they were my most treasured possessions. Lucie said again, 'Sell my pots – I can make you more.' So I was persuaded – and this led to a huge change in my life.

So where to sell Lucie's pots? I took three to Sotheby's and three to Christies. There was not a big market in modern ceramics at this time, but a limited number of pieces were included in decorative arts auctions. At Christies decorative arts were organised by a former ballet dancer called Sheila Harrison; there was no one there who had a knowledge of ceramics. Before long, with the support of her managing director, Paul Whitfield, Sheila suggested I join Christies as a consultant, for a small fee. This was to develop over the years as a major part of my life.

It was during this lean period that I was offered some commercials in Vienna – and a number for Manner chocolate biscuits: one in Stockholm, one in Paris, one in London and one in Vienna. They were very successful, so Unilever asked me to do one for Phillips televisions and a number of others, mainly for Unilever. Unilever was pleased to have an English director, and gave me lots of work, putting me up in the Sacher Hotel in the centre of Vienna. We advertised their hair products with the style -setting hairdressers the Bundy Brothers. Occasionally we had a guest star, Geraldine Chaplin or Elke Sommers, for example, but on the whole making commercials meant working with non-actors: again, my knowledge of voice and being truthful to yourself came into play.

Before making these commercials, I naturally asked who the cameraman was. I was told he was Heinz Lazek, a young man, which worried me. I went to meet him. We became friends instantly, and remain so to this day.

Permission to Kill, 1976

Heinz Lazek was later appointed managing director of state-sponsored Wien Film. In 1976 he and they invited me to make a feature film, a political thriller, in Vienna. It was a good script – an excellent script – by Robin Estridge, called *Permission to Kill*. Dirk Bogarde and Ava Gardner were the stars, together with a young Timothy Dalton. Again I had a great cameraman, Freddie Young – one of the greatest. We became more than brothers. I had such respect for him. Freddie and I would walk round the set and I'd say, 'I think the shot should be from here,' and so on and so forth; this might be a week before we were doing that shot. But he would remember, and he'd go and put the camera there and say, 'That's where you said you wanted it.' I remember one scene on a boat, with a child. I rehearsed quietly with the child and surprised Freddie by saying I wanted a close up. He couldn't believe it, just couldn't believe that the boy could express such emotion in a close-up. That was one of my great experiences, working with him.

Working with Ava Gardner, whom I adored, was also a great experience. She was a beautiful lady and a marvellous person. It was Dirk Bogarde who suggested her for the part. When I first met her about the film – she'd been in my restaurant many times for dinner, but not as my guest – she said, 'You know I can't act.' I said, 'Don't worry, I'm with you.' And of course she was a delight. A photo from her is still on my mantelpiece today, with the inscription: 'Darling Cornflakes, thanks for making work a joy. Love you, Ava.'

Ava always called me 'Cornflakes'. One day I called at her hotel in Vienna, and she had a very nice dresser with her, Renee (who later wrote a book in which she tells this story). I rang up and said I wanted to see Ms Gardner. Renee said, 'Who is it?' I said, 'Cyril.' And she said to Ava, 'It's Cereal' – and Ava fell about laughing. Then they both fell about laughing, saying, 'Oh, it's Cornflakes,' and from then on I was Cornflakes.

Ava was originally put up in the Sacher Hotel. One evening she went out for a little stroll down the main street. The night porter refused to let her back in, thinking she was a prostitute. She fled and went to the Hilton, and later the Bristol Hotel. I always felt the Sacher was a hotel run for the benefit of the staff and not for the guests.

I was enchanted with Ava and we became great friends. She lived in London – Ennismore Gardens, just off Hyde Park – and I used to join her walking her dog in the park. In September 1980 Sinatra came over for a concert and sent her two complimentary tickets, but she wouldn't go because he'd come over with some blonde girl and gave me the tickets. Throughout the concert Sinatra sang to me – in the centre gangway of the circle – thinking that's where she was sitting.

The Return of the Saint, 1977

I did one more film (for TV) in the '70s before moving to an almost permanent residency in Vienna as a theatre director. *The Return of the Saint* was a two-parter, also shown as a single feature. I think the invitation came from Robert Baker. The original *Saint* had been produced by Bob Baker and Monty Berman, who had produced *Gideon's Way*, of which I had directed several episodes.

The lead was played by Ian Ogilvy, and I invited one of my favourite actresses to play alongside him, Stephanie Beacham, who was a great pleasure to work with. We had locations in the south of France and it was a very happy shoot. The only problem was that the script was slow to arrive, so Dennis Spooner and I agreed that I would improvise situations and he would use the material to build the scripts around. Again I didn't plan whole days in advance: I needed to know three shots – the one before, the one now and the one to follow. I've maintained that thinking ever since. Three is the magic number.

When I returned from location I was offered more television, *The New Avengers*, but I turned it down. I said no: apart from the feeling that I'd done it, for ten years and countless episodes, the quality of writing was hard to get enthusiastic about. I remember on one earlier shoot when I received a script with a lot of problems. There was a lot wrong with it. I went to the script editor and said, 'I've got four major points – I want this changed, and that . . .' And he turned to me and said, 'Cyril, why are you making complications? It's only for television.' So I put things right myself, made it interesting . . . and when the producers saw it they said, 'You see, there was nothing wrong with it after all.'

I'd had a wonderful film career, and although I didn't see myself as withdrawing from it, it was time to do something different.

Chapter 9

Theatre in Vienna & Documentaries at the BBC 1977–1983

The assistant director on the film I made in Germany in the early '60s, *Grounds for Divorce: Love* was an Israeli named Abraham. He had introduced me to his parents, and I was fed and treated like family at his home. As well as showing me some of the more colourful haunts of Berlin, Abraham had introduced me to an Austrian professor and writer named Adolf Opel. A little later Opel went to the English Theatre in Vienna and told them they should use Cyril Frankel. Over the next seven years I directed some twenty plays, which I proposed, mainly at the English Theatre and the Josefstadt (Max Reinhardt's theatre) but also several English comedies at Kleine Komodie, Vienna and Komodie Theatre, Frankfurt. The director of the English Theatre said, 'You've been making films. Can you bring some "names" to Vienna?'

The productions included Simon Gray's *Otherwise Engaged* (1977), Joe Orton's *What the Butler Saw*, Frederick Knott's *Dial M for Murder* and many more. Noel Coward's *Relative Values* starred Dame Anna Neagle. Anna was of course a huge star back home, but not so celebrated in Vienna – though her performance in the play was widely praised and appreciated by full houses. Constance Cummings starred in George Bernard Shaw's *Mrs Warren's Profession*. She was a consummate actress of great beauty. After the first night she asked why I wasn't directing in London's West End. I said that I hadn't been asked . . . yet.

In 1980 I directed Joan Fontaine in James Goldman's *The Lion in Winter*. I thought of Joan for the part, and when I telephoned her and said it was *The Lion in Winter* she immediately replied that she'd love to as she was descended from the Plantagenets. We rented a very nice flat for her on the Ring, but she had a bad experience with a lift so she moved to a hotel. Joan was wonderful and of course a big attraction to the Vienna audience, although I recall the director of the theatre had a wife who was jealous of her, and invited her to a lunch where no one spoke English.

Ben Toff advised me to have a 'star lift' on Joan's entrance. When I asked him what he meant he said, 'Make sure that before her entrance your overall lighting is moderate, and then on her entrance lift everything up.' It certainly worked. I also choreographed the curtain call, an effective addition to the play – and word spread of its entertainment value. A butler character opened doors to reveal the actors in turn: Joan's door was at the top of a staircase, which she came down to great applause.

I directed Frederick Knott's *Wait Until Dark* four times. It was a tremendous hit and I was asked to take it to Munich as well, where it was an even bigger hit; I was invited back to direct Ira Levin's *Death Trap*. The other two productions were in Basingstoke and Woking. One of these, unfortunately, led to the souring of my relationship with Peter Wyngarde, who had performed in a number of my television series, including the lead in *Jason King*. Peter would not take direction, insisting on making an entrance before the female lead and in my opinion spoiling the second half of the play.

In Joseph Kesselring's *Arsenic and Old Lace*, which I envisaged as a wartime reflection on attitudes to death, I cast the two *grande dames* of Vienna theatre. A Swiss actor played the role that Cary Grant plays in the film. I was blessed with a superb set by Wolfgang Muller-Karbach, who did most of the sets for my plays.

Michael Frayn's *Noises Off* was perhaps one of the highlights of my life. The author came over to Vienna to see it and said it was better than the productions in New York and London. To improve on such a success was unbelievable. Casting, again, was key. That moment, that first performance, when the cast clicks – it rarely happens in a film studio – is so tremendous. And that moment when you're called onto the stage – and it's as though the whole auditorium is gold – is quite extraordinary. The

Austrian version of *Noises Off* ran and ran and ran and ran. I got medals for its performances, which led to more and more stage work in Vienna and Germany.

I was very lucky to have Elizabeth Fischer as my assistant in Vienna, for the commercials, films and theatre work. Her husband was a producer on Vienna television and social life was fun. The Bundy brothers, whom I had worked with on the Unilever commercials, remained good friends, and they found me a lovely penthouse apartment on the Ring, a very fine home from home. Hans Bundy and his wife, who was a ballet mistress, also lived on the Ring, in an apartment entirely decorated with Art Deco; I was regularly invited to dine with them.

Ironically it was at this time, when I was spending months at a time away from England, that I secured the home in Harley Street that has been my permanent base every since. My uncle Mark had a lease for the house for a matter of only twenty-three years or so. It had been bombed during the war and the upper part had been rebuilt. Originally a family house, it was now broken into flats, all of which were controlled tenancies. In 1980 the person who was in the first-floor flat married and had a child, and he and his wife wanted a bigger place. He wanted to pass it over to a friend but my uncle said that he wanted a member of his family there. At that time I was in a little flat near Marylebone High Street – Weymouth Mews – and he said, oh you're much better off coming to Harley Street. And it was only once I was in and my uncle died at the age of ninety-four, that I negotiated with the estate and surrendered what was left of my lease, which was something like seven years, for ninety-nine years – which is when I had the offer for my collection of pots, thus enabling me to do this. So I acquired a ninety-nine year lease for a relatively reasonable sum of money, considering what it's worth even in today's market.

I moved in, and was soon joined by Steve Nelson, to whom I'd been introduced by my great friend Irving Davis. Over a period of time Steve and I had become good friends. Steve had been born in Aldershot, his father being in the Army, and was raised in south London, but his parents had later moved to Worthing. Steve was living in Soho, but fell out with the people he was living with and turned up on the doorstep here – I'd said come anytime – and we've been close companions ever since. We are now even civil partners. I regard him as a kind of angel sent down to look after me, which is what he does.

BBC Documentaries

I'd been a friend of Lucie Rie since 1954. She was approaching eighty and Sir Robert and Lady Lisa Sainsbury were planning an exhibition to celebrate the occasion at their marvellous Sainsbury Centre for Visual Arts at the University of East Anglia, which contains their wonderful collection of paintings and antiques, assembled over many years. I had been asked to lend some of my pots. When I woke one morning my mind was filled with the thought that because my dear friend Lucie was having this exhibition I should make a film about her and her work. Obviously it should be made by the BBC, but I knew no one there. I picked up the telephone and, without difficulty, got straight through to the Head of Music and Arts, Richard Somerset-Ward, and a meeting with him was arranged at the Music and Arts Department at Shepherds Bush. I told him I wanted to make a programme about Lucie Rie. He said they'd always wanted to film her but she wouldn't agree to being filmed. I explained that I was a close friend and I felt she would agree. He responded, 'If you can bring Lucie Rie, we'll make it. If you speak to *Omnibus* and *Arena* we'll go ahead with whichever says yes.'

It took three weeks to gain entry to Christopher Martin, who was in charge of *Omnibus*. He said that if I could bring Lucie then *Omnibus* would be delighted. I hurried back to Albion Mews, where Lucie lived and worked. She opened the door and said, 'Cyril, you'll never guess who was just here. John Schlesinger. He wants to make a film about me. I told him over my dead body!' I told her I'd just been to the BBC. 'Cyril, you know I hate being photographed. No, no, no!' I was deeply disappointed, knowing in my heart that this film was vital as a permanent record of Lucie and her work. But she was adamant and we agreed not to talk about it further.

I visited her regularly at this stage and about three weeks later, on my way to her front door, I was met by Janet Leach, Bernard's widow, who whispered to me, 'I think she's changing her mind! She'll tell you.' So I went in and we went straight upstairs for coffee. Lucie said, 'Now, about this film . . .' 'But we said we'd never talk about it.' She answered, 'Both Hans [Coper] and Max Mayer [her doctor] think I'm stopping you from working for the BBC, which you've always wanted to do.' I replied that this was true . . . and so she agreed. And I agreed in turn that if there was something in the film she didn't like I'd cut it out.

Thrilled, I immediately contacted Christopher Martin of *Omnibus*. I planned to make the film at the Sainsbury Centre, where John Houston of the Arts Council was preparing the exhibition, and in Lucie's studio in Albion Mews. The next question was who should interview her. I discussed this problem with my friend Phivos Petrou and he suggested David Attenborough: we'd seen him at exhibition openings at the Casson Gallery in Marylebone High Street. I spoke to *Omnibus*, as I knew David was producing his nature series for them, and said I knew that David and his delightful wife Jane were both collectors and admirers of Lucie. Unfortunately David was in the Antarctic, and said he'd only be available for two days. I worked out how I could, as it were, film around him.

When I told Lucie that David had agreed to interview her, she was really pleased. 'He always makes me laugh!' she said. Filming went very smoothly. The cameraman, Philip Bonham Carter, was totally at one with me and we worked with a minimum crew. The climax came with Lucie opening her kiln to unload her fired pots. On several previous occasions she had asked me over to help her do this, so I knew she would bend over the top of the kiln and ask for her legs to be held. I warned David about this and told Philip to keep the camera running whatever happened. Then I simply prayed for it to happen – and it did.

The film was beautifully edited by Phil Wrestler, who had been second unit director on *The Italian Job* and was companion to my dear friend and colleague Anne Deeley. When I showed the fine cut to Lucie in a Wardour Street cutting room she liked it, but said that I was to cut out the undignified bit where she unloaded the kiln. I explained that when David responded to her 'Would you hold my legs, please?' was the emotional heart of the whole film – but Lucie replied, 'Cyril, you promised you would cut out anything I didn't like.' I had to think hard, and told her we'd run the film for a crowd of her friends – and that if anyone found the sequence undignified I'd cut it out.

I hired the cinema at the British Film Academy and about thirty people came. They all congratulated her, particularly for the kiln sequence. She came up to me, grasped my arm and said, 'You can keep it in.' The film was a great success for *Omnibus* and was shown a second time when BBC4 was inaugurated, to coincide with Lucie's centenary, with a new introduction by me and Conran. So it lives on.

After the Lucy Rie film the BBC asked if there was anyone else I knew who was impossible. I replied that, as a matter of fact, there was . . .

At the end of the war I was touring the Berlin Philharmonic Orchestra with the conductor Sergei Celibidache, who had taken over from Furtwangler. 'Celi' later travelled to various countries, and in the mid-'50s came to London to conduct the London Philharmonic. His creative conducting truly produced music more flowing and vibrant than ever before. He utterly believed in the living experience and absolutely refused to make recordings. Christopher Martin said, 'Well, if you can get him . . .'

I'd last seen Celibidache many years before when, together with John and Susan Allison and Michael Frostick, we'd spent several evenings discussing Buddhism. Now in the early 1980s – some thirty years after we had first met – I knew he was living with his wife and son in Paris. Christopher agreed I should visit him and persuade him to be filmed, so I contacted him and went to his apartment. Almost the first thing he said to me was that he had moved on from Buddhism to become a disciple of the Hindu Sai Baba, and visited India regularly. When I mentioned making a film he turned to his lovely wife and said, 'I've known Cyril for some thirty years. I can trust him.' He told me he was soon to conduct the London Symphony Orchestra in London, and we could film the rehearsals of Fauré's *Requiem*.

The result was a one-hour *Omnibus* that was nominated for an Emmy. The BBC was thrilled: 'the controller of BBC1 has asked me to convey his appreciation and thanks for establishing *Omnibus* as an important vehicle for the Arts'. The film was nominated as the BBC's entry for the Prix Italia, and I received this from Alan Harte, then controller of BBC1: 'I felt this was a magnificent, enthralling programme and tremendous triumph for *Omnibus* . . . Congratulations to all concerned in the making.' And this from Richard Somerset-Ward, head of Music and Arts:

> Dear Cyril,
> It was splendid to see the Celibidache film finally go on the air on Sunday. You will have seen the reviews which are unanimous, I think. So far reaction here – that's the BBC – it has won sustained plaudits from all the senior programme people including the whole

of the review board . . . And I think it has a
genuine chance of regaining the Prix which
we won for the first time last year . . . Many
congratulations and many thanks to you.

Christopher Martin and I travelled to New York for the Emmy
ceremony and I put forward my next BBC idea, which was to film
the story of Celia Franca's brilliant creation of the National Ballet
of Canada in Toronto. Celia had been in Canada since 1950. Two
Canadian ladies had come to London to see Ninette de Valois,
director of the Royal Ballet, of which Celia was a member, and
asked her who they should invite to Canada to start their
National Ballet. Ninette had immediately responded that they
should get Franca – which they did.

So after New York Christopher and I flew to Toronto. Celia –
now a First Lady of Canada, the equivalent of a Dame – agreed,
and the film *Bold Steps* was made. Again this film went down
very well, and it won a prize in Italy, at the Padua Film
Festival.

I wasn't successful in persuading all my friends to be part of
this series for the BBC. When I went to Kenya to suggest it to
Maharishi, he refused . . . but he did say I could make a film for
him – which I did, but it hasn't been widely seen.

My next programme for the BBC was a documentary about
the Old Vic – about Lilian Baylis and 'Honest Ed', the Canadian
discount store owner who had bought the theatre in the 1980s.
When I got a message that Ralph Richardson wanted to meet the
director I went to his home: he'd moved from Hampstead to one
of those terraces on Regent's Park. When I got into the hallway
he was standing at the top of the stairs. 'Oh, it's you! I didn't
need to meet you!' This was his very last performance in
anything. In November 1983 Ian Squires, head of *Omnibus*, wrote
to me: 'Dear Cyril, Excuse the formality of the note, but Richard
Somerset-Ward has just told me that the Old Vic received an 'A1'
of 79 [that's the scale by which the audience researchers judge
the viewer's reaction to a programme]. Richard tells me this is
extremely high and wished me to pass on even more
congratulations.'

My last programme was about Martin Bloch, a favourite artist
of mine who had died in 1954. It was his centenary, but nobody
was doing anything. Recently I've helped to put on an exhibition
of his paintings at the Sainsbury Centre.

This was a wonderful period, mainly because the films were part autobiographical. And then, unfortunately, the BBC changed character and the Music and Arts Department was disbanded.

Chapter 10

Contemporary Ceramics 1984–2001

Christies

n the 1970s Lucie Rie had suggested that I become her
consultant and do all her pricing for her, as she never knew
the price of anything. It was at the time when the
restaurant finally had to close, and I had nowhere to live
because the lease of this huge house I had in Belgravia was up
and a new lease would involve me getting into a great deal of
debt. Lucie insisted, and her accountant insisted, on paying me –
which I resisted, but eventually accepted.

This, aside from my friendship with Lucie, led to the film
about her – which in turn led to me being invited by Christies to
become a consultant on studio pottery, as it was known. I
changed its name to contemporary ceramics, and I'm now
regarded as the principal authority in this field.

I realised that it was essential to establish these pots as works
of art, which had to be done not at auction but in conjunction with
museums. I organised major exhibitions at the Sainsbury Centre
and, together with Issey Miyake, at two museums in Japan. I was
the curator for a major Rie/Cooper exhibition at the Metropolitan
Museum, New York, and more recently curated a Lucie Rie
retrospective at Mak, Vienna. Lucie wouldn't have anything to do
with Vienna. When I suggested an exhibition in the museum there
she said, 'You can do it when I'm dead.' So I did.

It was through Lucie that I met Sir Robert and Lady
Sainsbury, and I received much encouragement from them. The

first time I witnessed them responding to a work of art was at a gallery in Motcom Street, where they were both musing over a Hans Coper vessel. They both reached the same conclusion – and when Lucie invited me to accompany her to dinner at their home I was delighted to see the Coper residing on the mantelpiece. (Also present on that occasion was Peter Palumbo, who over a period of time became a good friend of mine.) I have regularly witnessed the extraordinary unity of mind between Sir Robert and Lady Sainsbury over works of art. They were delighted when I brought glass cases into my auctions at Christies and staged the sales more in the form of exhibitions. At my first ceramics exhibition they chose and agreed upon a handsome vase, which later sat proudly on a side table in their entrance hall.

Lady Sainsbury has constantly sought out talent and encouraged the young. She has focused on assisting artists who are in one way or another in need, providing them with a studio to work in or with introductions to promote their work, not only in London but also in New York, Japan and all around the world. The list of those she has helped is long, and continues to grow.

I curated several exhibitions and events for the Sainsburys, and in 2000 published *Modern Pots* (Thames and Hudson), describing Lady Sainsbury's collection. The second edition of this has now been published. Other activities have included exhibitions of photography – including images of Marilyn Monroe, photographs by Eve Arnold and the Magnum photographers – and an exhibition of Martin Bloch paintings, which has gone to the National Gallery of Wales.

The encouragement of Lady Sainsbury has been instrumental in my success in this field: she has been a constant encouragement and support. I love her. In gratitude I've donated my memorabilia of Lucie Rie and three of my Martin Blochs to the Sainsbury Centre at the University of East Anglia.

Returning to Film

In 1990 I went back to Germany to make one more film, called *Eine Frau Namens Harry*. It was called *Harry and Harriet* at first, but was changed to *Eine Frau Namens Harry* because the leading actor, Thomas Gottschalk, was such a big noise in Germany. I can't think of anybody in England who has as big a name on television. It was a simple story of a girl who was unhappy being a girl, who tries to commit suicide and is then confronted by the devil – Charles Gray – who turns her into a man. The film was shot in English, although they never finished the English version and it was dubbed into German. The female stars were Fiona Fullerton and Stephanie Beecham – this is from Stephanie, 'Thank you for a wonderful time . . . Again. Soon. Please.' *Eine Frau Namens Harry* was very successful in Germany.

Bonhams

The man who took me on at Christies was Paul Whitfield, the managing director. When he moved to Bonhams he invited me to join him – but it took over a year because he couldn't take anyone with him from Christies.

It was at Bonhams that I really went to town. The first big pottery sale, their accountant Heather Ramsey told me, was their only sale in memory where they sold 100 per cent. Christopher Elwes, managing director of Bonhams, wrote:

> Dear Cyril,
> I hope you are coming back down to earth.
> Last night was a tremendous personal success for you as well as for Bonhams. Such a result only comes from hard work, dedication and professionalism – and in this you set a great example to the rest of Bonhams, as well as providing us with a great morale boost. Very many thanks and very well done.
> Yours, Christopher.

At the beginning of April 2000 Sir Robert Sainsbury died. Robert and Lisa had been enchanted by my Celibidache film, and in writing to me of their enjoyment, Lisa told me that she had written into her will that I should stage a performance of Fauré's *Requiem* as her memorial – but when Sir Robert passed away first she changed her mind. We should do it for Bob, she told me, and we did – with the City of London Sinfonia, conducted by Harry Christophers, at St John's, Smith Square – a concert in celebration of the life of Sir Robert Sainsbury. Their son David, the present Lord Sainsbury, wrote to me:

> Dear Cyril,
> I was very moved by the concert to celebrate the life of my father and would like to thank

you for all the help you gave in arranging it. As you know my father liked everything to be done with care and thoughtfulness and to the highest standards and I know that he would have loved the programme of *Faure's Requiem*. It's a wonderful piece of music and I thought that the performance of it that you arranged was very beautiful. The people that you got to perform were outstanding and they rose to the special nature of the occasion and the beauty of the building. From the comments people made I know that they greatly appreciated the opportunity to reflect on the life of my father and to hear such wonderful music and would like me to convey to you our thanks as well as my own for making possible such a memorable performance.

Best wishes, David.

Phillips

From Bonhams I moved to Phillips. It was while I was there that I received a letter from Christopher Frayling, who is now head of the Arts Council but was then Head of the Royal College of Art. He said they wanted me to accept the Honorary Fellowship of the Royal College of Art. When I went to see him, I said, by the way, your father and my father were great friends. And he said, 'What, Manny Frankel? I *knew* this was going to be a good thing!'

Lucie's death

Lucie Rie was ninety-three when she died on 1 April 1995. As I have said, I was a regular visitor to Albion Mews. Shortly before she died I recall her asking me to get some ground hazelnuts, as she had promised to make somebody a cake. I went round one morning to deliver these and, on entering the mews, met the couple who lived opposite the studio, Michael Simonow and his Japanese wife. They told me that Lucie had had a stroke and was now in hospital. I sped to St Mary's to see her, but very soon she was back home, where she was tended by three Australian nurses – arranged by Lady Sainsbury. I visited every day.

Lucie had always been independent. Needing nurses was frustrating for her, and contrary to her desire to control her own affairs. So she made an inner decision, and refused to take either food or water. I continued to visit, holding her hand and stroking her brow, releasing tensions – but her refusal to take any liquid or food continued.

The March weather became more and more dark and overcast, and it frequently poured with rain. One day the nurses, accustomed to my regular visits, phoned and said that they thought I should come. So I hurried over, with a dark and threatening sky above, and went to Lucie's side. At one point the nurse said, 'She's changing colour.' I continued to hold her hand, and suddenly a golden ray of sun broke through the clouds and a beam of light centred on the mews. The nurse and I were both astounded, and instinctively went down into the mews – where I experienced a vision: a great throne speeding Lucie up the ray of light and into the sun.

When we returned to the apartment Lucie, quite simply, was not there.

How extraordinary it is that so many of the people I have encountered have an 'aura' around them. Being in touch with the inner spirit, I believe, produces vibrations that give this aura.

I recalled how I asked Maharishi how one should prepare for death. He responded with laughter and said, 'Human beings are so funny. Don't they realise that death is a joyful thing, as it frees the spirit to escape the prison of the body?' And he said, as always, 'Jai Guru Dev' – 'Bless the Divine Course'.

And there we are – I'm now in my eighties and I'm enjoying life. It's been a very rich life. Oh, it has. I was born lucky . . .

Filmography

1953 *Man of Africa*

1954 *Devil on Horseback*

1954 *Make Me an Offer*

1956 *It's Great to Be Young!*

1957 *No Time for Tears*

1958 *She Didn't Say No!*

1959 *Alive and Kicking*

1960 *Never Take Sweets from a Stranger*
aka *Never Take Candy from a Stranger*

1960 *School for Scoundrels* (uncredited)
aka *School for Scoundrels or How to Win Without Actually Cheating!* (UK long title)

1960 *Scheidungsgrund: Liebe*
aka *Grounds For Divorce: Love*

1961 *On the Fiddle*
aka *Operation Snafu* (USA)
aka *Operation War Head* (USA: reissue title)

1961 *Don't Bother to Knock*
aka *Why Bother to Knock* (USA)

1962 *The Very Edge*

1965 *Gideon's Way* (6 episodes)
aka *Gideon CID* (USA)
Big Fish, Little Fish
Morna
The V Men
The Alibi Men
The Millionaire's Daughter
The Thin Red Line

1965 *The Man in a Looking Glass* (TV)

1966 *The Baron* (4 episodes)
Something for a Rainy Day (17 February 1966)
And Suddenly You're Dead (31 March 1966)
Masquerade (28 April 1966)
The Killing (5 May 1966)

1966 *The Witches* (1966)
aka *The Devil's Own* (USA)

1966 *The Trygon Factor* (1966)
aka *Factor One* (UK video title)
aka *Das Geheimnis der weißen Nonne*(West Germany)

1968 *The Avengers* (1 episode)
Whoever Shot Poor George/XR40?

1968– 9 *The Champions* (10 episodes)
The Beginning (25 September 1968)
The Invisible Man (2 October 1968)
Reply Box No. 666 (9 October 1968)
The Experiment (16 October 1968)
Happening (23 October 1968)
The Survivors (6 November 1968)
The Dark Island (4 December 1968)
The Gilded Cage (8 January 1969)
The Interrogation (5 February 1969)

Get Me Out of Here! (26 February 1969)

1969– 70 *Department S* (9 episodes)
Six Days (9 March 1969)
The Trojan Tanker (16 March 1969) – creative consultant
The Man in the Elegant Room (13 April 1969)
The Man Who Got a New Face (15 October 1969)
Les Fleurs du Mal (22 October 1969)
The Perfect Operation (26 November 1969)
The Mysterious Man in the Flying Machine (12 December 1969)
The Ghost of Mary Burnham (18 February 1970)
A Fish Out of Water (25 February 1970)
A Ticket to Nowhere (11 March 1970)

1969– 70 *Randall and Hopkirk (Deceased)* (6 episodes)
aka *My Partner the Ghost* (USA)
My Late Lamented Friend and Partner (21 September 1969)
A Disturbing Case (28 September 1969) – creative consultant
For the Girl Who Has Everything (7 December 1969)
Somebody Just Walked Over My Grave (9 January 1970)
The Ghost Talks (6 February 1970)
The Trouble with Women (20 February 1970)
Vendetta for a Dead Man (27 February 1970)

1971– 3 *UFO* (2 episodes)
Timelash (17 February 1971)
The Long Sleep (15 March 1973)

1971– 1972 *Jason King* (11 episodes)
Wanna buy a television series? (15 September 1971) – creative
    consultant
Variations on a Theme (20 October 1971)
A Red Red Rose Forever (1 December 1971)
All That Glisters: Part 1 (8 December 1971)
All That Glisters: Part 2 (15 December 1971)
Uneasy Lies the Head (19 January 1972)
Nadine (2 February 1972)
A Kiss for a Beautiful Killer (9 February 1972)
If It's Got to Go, It's Got to Go (16 February 1972)
    A Thin Band of Air (3 March 1972)
Every Picture Tells a Story (31 March 1972)
Chapter One: The Company I Keep (7 April 1972)

1972– 3 *The Adventurer* (13 episodes)
Counterstrike (1 January 1972) – creative consultant
Return to Sender (1 January 1972)
Target! (1 January 1972)
Deadlock (1 January 1972) – creative consultant
Has Anyone Here Seen Kelly? (1 January 1972) – creative
    consultant
The Bradley Way (1 January 1972) – creative consultant
Nearly the End of the Picture (1 January 1972)
Action! (1 January 1972) – creative consultant
Thrust and Counter Thrust (1 January 1972) – creative
    consultant
Love Always, Magda (1 January 1972)
Skeleton in the Cupboard (1 January 1972)
Poor Little Rich Girl (1 January 1972)
Miss Me Once, Miss Me Twice and Miss Me Once Again (29
    September 1972)
Somebody Doesn't Like Me (1 January 1973)
The Not-So Merry Widow (1 January 1973)
The Solid Gold Hearse (1 January 1973) – creative consultant
I'll Get There Sometime (1 January 1973) – creative consultant
Icons Are Forever (1 January 1973)
Double Exposure (1 January 1973)
The Good Book (1 January 1973)
The Case of the Poisoned Pawn (23 February 1973)

1972– 4 *The Protectors* (4 episodes)
Thinkback (24 November 1972)
Vocal (16 February 1973)
Petard (26 October 1973)
A Pocketful of Posies (22 February 1974)

1975 *Permission to Kill*
aka *The Executioner* (USA)

1979 *Return of the Saint* (2 episodes)
aka The Son of the Saint
Collision Course: The Brave Goose (7 January 1979)
Collision Course: The Sixth Man (14 January 1979)
1983 *Legend of the Champions* (TV)

1986 *Hammer House of Mystery and Suspense* (1 episode)
Tennis Court (9 May 1986)

Eine Frau namens Harry (Germany)
aka *Harry and Harriet* (1990) (USA)

Acknowledgements

Lady Lisa Sainsbury - for all her encouragement in all artistic matters, not only to me, but to all young creative people.

Henry Cobbold - for all his work creating this book.

Steve Nelson - for caring for me, a full-time responsibility since I have suffered several mini strokes.

Lightning Source UK Ltd.
Milton Keynes UK
01 May 2010

153612UK00001B/12/P